MASTERING
PASTORAL
COUNSELING

MASTERING
PASTORAL
COUNSELING

Archibald D. Hart
Gary L. Gulbranson
Jim Smith

MULTNOMAH

Portland, Oregon 97266

Christianity Today, Inc.

MASTERING PASTORAL COUNSELING
© 1992 by Christianity Today, Inc.
Published by Multnomah Press
10209 SE Division Street
Portland, Oregon 97266

Multnomah Press is a ministry of Multnomah School of the Bible, 8435 NE Glisan Street, Portland, Oregon 97220.

Printed in the United States of America.

Library of Congress Cataloging-in-Publication Data

Hart, Archibald D.
    Mastering pastoral counseling / Archibald Hart, Gary
   Gulbranson, James Smith.
      p. cm. — (Mastering ministry)
   ISBN 0-88070-486-1
   1. Pastoral counseling. I. Gulbranson, Gary. II. Smith, Jim.
 1936–   III. Title. IV. Series
 BV4012.2.H364 1992
 253.5—dc20   90-29000
                                 CIP

92 93 94 95 96 97 98 99 00 01 - 10 9 8 7 6 5 4 3 2 1

Contents

85098

Introduction

He called for a sword and ordered the baby to be cut in two. An incredible solution, but it worked.

From my perspective as a pastor, though, the puzzle Solomon faced that day was an easy call compared to the Gordian knots people brought to my office for counseling. The complexity of life and the rain-forest jungle that results from today's moral confusion is making pastoral counseling an increasingly challenging task.

Yet I think Solomon would have been up to it. Wisdom is a sharp machete. "A wise man has great power," said Solomon, "and a man of knowledge increases strength."

If there is one thing counseling pastors never have enough of, it's wisdom. Wisdom to peer through the shadowy underbrush of rationalizations, excuses, self-deception, and passions of the human heart — the heart only God can fully know. Wisdom to know when to talk and when to listen. Wisdom to sense how fast or slow to proceed, to sensitively employ spiritual resources, to balance counseling with other pastoral duties, to judge whether to refer or to provide help yourself, to know when to confront and when to support. Wisdom to provide, of all things, spiritual direction.

If there is one thing the three authors of this volume of Mastering Ministry have, it is wisdom, gained through much experience and considerable training.

Because of the sensitive nature of the illustrations that fill a book on counseling, we have modified the facts in the true stories in this book to protect the confidentiality and identity of those involved. But here are the unaltered facts about the three contributors.

Gary Gulbranson

The first time I phoned Gary Gulbranson, he was out of the office on an errand, so I talked with his secretary. Then she put me on hold.

A moment later, I heard a man's voice say, "Can I help you?" I inquired about Gary's schedule and availability, and finally suggested he might let Gary know about my call when he returned. He replied, "This is Gary Gulbranson."

All that to say, Gary is unassuming. When we went to his office to interview him for this book, his manner with us and the church staff clearly showed that he is approachable, attentive to those around him, a man of the people. He talks in brief idea packages that give ample time and space for your thoughts. Gary puts you at ease.

But the ministry demands he puts on himself are anything but easygoing. He pastors Glen Ellyn Bible Church, which has grown from 175 to 800 Sunday attenders since he came in 1983. The church recently completed a building expansion project. In addition, he's involved in community and Christian organizations — active in Rotary and serving on boards of institutions as diverse as a seminary and a savings and loan. He also teaches counseling at Moody Graduate School in Chicago.

Yet he doesn't let the many demands of ministry steal time away from meeting people one-on-one. He still carves out about fifteen counseling appointments each week.

Gary has earned an Ed.D. in educational psychology from Loyola University, an M.Div. from Denver Seminary, and a B.A. from Trinity College in Deerfield, Illinois.

Archibald Hart

One of my colleagues at LEADERSHIP tells me that after his first encounter with Arch Hart, he just wanted to get some sleep. That's because Arch, who was speaking at a minister's conference my friend was attending, had warned pastors about the relationship of adrenalin and stress, and had advocated perhaps the most effective anecdote: more sleep. My colleague recognized the symptoms, took the prescription, and, he tells me, has been a happier, more productive person since.

That is certainly a combination one sees in Arch: a productive and energetic life that shows few signs of stress and tension. He began his professional career as a civil engineer in South Africa. After earning a Ph.D. at the University of Natal in South Africa, he began a private counseling practice. He came to Fuller Theological Seminary in 1973, and now serves there as dean of the graduate school of psychology. He's a popular conference speaker. He's written many articles for professional and popular journals, and he's authored a dozen books, among them *The Hidden Link Between Adrenalin and Stress*, *Unlocking the Mystery of Your Emotions*, *Counseling the Depressed*, and most recently, *Healing Adult Children of Divorce*.

Amidst all this, he finds time to get a full night's sleep!

Arch also finds time to counsel, and many of his clients have been pastors. He knows not only the tensions pastors face but also the counseling situations that most challenge them.

Jim Smith

Entering Jim's office in Dallas' Highland Park Presbyterian Church, one is immediately aware of his love of the outdoors: the walls are covered with hunting and fishing trophies. His weekly Thursday treks into the wilderness have allowed Jim to bag some big ones.

When he sits at his desk, a huge wild turkey, with wings outstretched, looms over his head from the wall behind. "They are the toughest thing you can hunt," says Jim. "They're smart, and they're fast. If they see even the smallest motion from you, they're gone before you can get the gun to your shoulder." That's why Jim likes to hunt them.

Tough but delicate challenges are one of the things that draw him to counseling as well. Based on the demand for his counseling — his schedule is full months in advance — he obviously is meeting the challenge.

Jim Smith graduated *magna cum laude* from Morris Harvey College (now the University of Charleston). He's had extensive experience with Youth for Christ, serving eventually as area vice-president for eleven states.

Jim came to Highland Park Presbyterian Church in 1973 as director of Christian education. In 1983 he assumed the responsibility of executive director of the Family Life Counseling Center, an extension of the ministry of the church. He is also author of *Learning to Live with the One You Love* (Tyndale, 1992).

As a pastor, I regarded counseling as my Achilles heel. I have always been far more interested in preaching than counseling, so I expected to be less than energized by working with these men.

Instead, I've learned more from them than from all my counseling training and experience put together. The coup de grace: their combined wisdom has left me with a palpable feeling of confidence about counseling that I never had before.

I'll leave it to your judgment whether these three men have a good measure of the wisdom of Solomon.

— Craig Brian Larson
associate editor, LEADERSHIP
Carol Stream, Illinois

PART ONE

The Pastor as Counselor

Spiritual resources for counseling, though not automatically effective, are, when used with wisdom, supernaturally effective.

— Gary Gulbranson

CHAPTER ONE

Using Our Spiritual Resources

For over a year I counseled a woman whose problems stemmed primarily from abuse. Throughout her life she had been physically and emotionally mistreated by various men, including her husband. In order to find personal healing and wholeness in her marriage, she desperately needed the spiritual resource of biblical truth.

In our early sessions, however, I knew I couldn't simply read the blueprint for wedded peace in Ephesians 5, not because I doubted the validity of that passage in her difficult situation but because she would not understand those verses as God intends. For her the term *submit* had been perverted into *be abused*.

Still, I had to offer her spiritual resources. The question was how.

Like a surgeon at a state-of-the-art hospital who employs the best technology can offer, a Christian counselor has powerful resources — spiritual resources — to draw on, but they are not automatically helpful. They can even be counterproductive. Over the years, I've learned that a counselor must employ spiritual resources with skill, sensitivity, and wisdom. Here is what I have discovered about their proper and beneficial use.

Use Prayer Intentionally

More than any other activity, prayer represents the spiritual side of counseling. Our prayers show we do not ultimately rely on our education, skills, or methods but on God's Spirit to work in this situation. Prayer is a confession of weakness that allows God's power to prevail.

Yet prayer can be unspiritual, even a counseling cop-out. A counselor may simply use prayer to produce an emotional catharsis. Or as a convenient way to bring ritual closure to a session — indeed to get rid of someone. Such tactics just cheapen prayer and disillusion the counselee about its effectiveness. Needy people desperately need a model of authentic prayer.

In counseling, prayer can be legitimate. Here's how I use it:

● *I pray before a session to prepare my attitude.* I occasionally have an adverse emotional bias about the situation of the counselee. As the father of two daughters, for instance, I have a tough time counseling a man guilty of child abuse. I pray for the compassion of Christ, for sensitivity concerning people's needs and what causes their behavior, for self-control so that I will not overreact.

● *I pray for guidance and insight.* My best insights into the puzzle of an individual's problems have come from the Holy Spirit. I've been trained to draw information out of people, and God uses that information to help them, but he sometimes reveals things to me that I couldn't have known or figured out myself. More often than not this will come in the form of an impression that suggests to me what trail to pursue.

A woman who had been sporadically attending our church with her husband and daughter called one day to request an appointment for herself and her husband. I asked if she could sketch her situation over the phone. "We have some business and marriage problems," she said.

On the day of their appointment, I prayed beforehand for guidance. "Lord, I sense a lot of things need to be dealt with here, and I need to handle them in their proper order. I'm not sure what that order should be. I need insight so that we can make enough progress to keep them working on their problems."

As the counseling session began and we got better acquainted, I felt a strong impression to pursue the business problem first. Bringing that up was like popping open a well-shaken Pepsi can. They had gone into business as husband and wife along with another family member. Along the way they had compromised their integrity.

We called a lawyer and set them on course to rectify matters. That brought immediate relief, enabling us in future sessions to resolve their marriage difficulties. The business situation had been the 400-horsepower engine of their conflict and pressure.

● *I pray with the counselee at the start of the counseling session.* In praying, I am communicating to God and to the counselee that I will draw on my relationship with the Lord to help this person. In addition, the counselee gains some sense of God's presence; it's not just the two of us in this office. As Alcoholics Anonymous and the recovery groups have proven, people who feel helpless or short on control need their attention drawn to God.

Such prayer changes the tone of the session. Many counselees are tense. Never having been through the counseling process, they are uncertain and vulnerable. But prayer relaxes them, as Philippians 4:6-7 promises, giving them a measure of the peace of God, which helps us communicate better.

● *I assign prayer as homework.* During marriage counseling, I always request that a husband and wife pray together at home. Prayer fosters an intimacy that cannot be produced any other way. In addition, they will get more in touch with their feelings in other facets of their lives. If they say they can't pray together, I suggest they talk about what they need and then pray silently in each other's presence.

I often use prayer as a homework assignment for the person who says, "I don't feel close to God. I just can't talk to him about this." I want such people to discover that we act our way into a proper way of feeling; we don't feel our way into a proper way of acting.

● *I pray to close the session.* This serves as a summary statement in God's presence, a reinforcement for the counselee that we've discussed this in God's presence, that he has heard what we've said, that he knows everything about them and the situation, that he cares more than I ever can. Especially when major sin is involved, people need to sense this bonding with God after they have brought their problems and failings into the open.

At this time I specifically ask God to work in the situation, to provide what is needed, to change what needs changing. This also conveys a message: I expect God actually to *do* something in their lives.

The nature of my relationship with the counselee determines who voices the closing prayer. Some people walk into my office with such a feeling of isolation or pride that the furthest thing from their mind is the possibility of praying with others about their problems. For them it's daunting enough just to talk about it. But with time they usually see prayer as something they want to share in.

● *I let counselees pray for me.* At the end of a session some counselees ask if they can pray for me, a sign, I think, of growing health. Especially because I relate with most of these people in the church context as well, I want them to know this is not a one-way street; I am receptive to what they want to return spiritually. I don't stay behind a big desk or pulpit, telling them how to straighten out their lives; I'd rather we share in ministry as members of the body of Christ.

Two steps out of my office, they are free to use their spiritual gifts. No matter how devastated at the moment, despite the present feelings of impotence, they can still do something significant for others: they can pray.

In dealing with the weighty, sometimes crushing problems of counseling, I have found, as a complement to prayer, that fasting is helpful. I don't assign it to counselees, but I fast for my own sake, when I need an emotional and spiritual bath. I also use it as a prayer discipline when dealing with a battery of problems that begin to affect my life, when counseling, for example, a host of people in marital crises and I'm starting to feel pressure in my own marriage. I use fasting to focus my attention on some aspect of God's character and simplify my desires.

Use Scripture Only After Understanding

In the confusion of their circumstances, hurting people desperately need and want wisdom and words from God. So a pastoral counselor has an incomparable spiritual resource: biblical truth. Scripture is my greatest counseling source for answers, comfort, and guidance.

But, like prayer, Scripture can be misused in counseling, and with greater harm. I can use the Bible in a way that short-circuits the counseling process. The counselee describes a few symptoms of her problem, and immediately verses begin popping into my mind. Before she can finish her story, I want to interrupt with last month's sermon on "How to Mend Your Marriage."

If I'm trigger-happy with Scripture, I'll fail to hear counselees' true concerns. As a result I won't understand their problems' contexts and causes.

Most important, I won't grasp how *they* understand the Bible. I can't hit the target unless I know what the target is. If I go too quickly to "thus saith the Lord" before I know what saith the counselee, I won't see what the real issues are. So I have found that I have to be patient at drawing people out. That being said, here is how I employ the Bible in counseling.

● *Use Scripture not to condemn but to outline a new direction.* This is how Jesus used the Word as he ministered to those who were sincere. Christ's use of Scripture differed radically from the Pharisees, who used Scripture to condemn people. They focused on the past, the sins already committed, and how God's commandments condemned such conduct.

Christ focused on the present and the future, on how a person could restore his relationship with God and how to maintain that relationship. With the woman caught in adultery, he refused to condemn but rather said, "Go your way and sin no more." Most people know when they are breaking God's plan. The resulting destruction eventually forces them to face the need for change.

Jesus was also sensitive to each individual. He understood people intimately and used Scripture in accordance with that insight. He helped people understand their motives and attitudes. Then he offered forgiveness, a fresh start, and a new discipline.

With the woman whose husband was abusing her, I had to first build trust, to let her relate to a masculine authority figure who did not abuse or manipulate her. We dealt with her past, helping her find comfort and healing.

When we came around to discussing her marriage, we began talking about submission. I made it clear that she had no obligation to submit to abuse, but I instructed her that the biblical model for marriage did require her to respect her husband in every way possible.

She went back to her home and did her best to implement what we talked about. It made a difference. Recently her husband dedicated his life to Christ, and they are beginning to develop a healthy marriage.

● *Back into Scripture.* Several years ago a husband and wife came for counseling. The wife's biggest complaint was "My husband isn't romantic enough." What he heard her saying, though, was "He's not good enough in bed." With such a narrow perspective on the term *romantic,* he was devastated, because he had been raised to take great pride in his ability to perform sexually.

I explored her complaint and discovered she was really saying, "He isn't attentive to me during the day." She had simple expectations: she wanted her husband to phone once a day from work to show that he cared what was happening in her life. In addition, she wanted to go out on a date once a month — with him arranging childcare. But she had never communicated this clearly.

I sat down with the husband and broadened his understanding of "romance," and things quickly improved between them.

People understand terms, including biblical terms, based on their experience. Until I understand their reference points, their context, their definitions, I will often miss the mark with Scripture. In fact most of the time, if I start with the Bible, telling people to "love" or "submit to one another" or "serve one another" without probing how they understand these biblical ideas, they end up feeling frustrated and condemned.

Often, after I've discovered what the counselee means by certain biblical phrases, I'll explain what the phrase means in its context, using their understanding by way of contrast. In addition, I try to help people discover the truth of Scripture for themselves: I assign homework, having them fill out worksheets on appropriate topics, such as abuse, alcohol, or marriage and family, which I've developed over the years.

Use Small Groups Strategically

A pastoral counselor can employ the home-field advantage: the church community. Pastors lead a group of people with the potential to serve and love others into well-being. But since such groups can easily turn into quagmires of dysfunction, I lead the groups in strategic ways.

● *I supervise involvement.* I don't just send people to support groups or ask them to get involved in Bible studies without watching over them as they get involved. And some people I will discourage altogether from small groups, at least until they can participate in them maturely.

Some individuals hug their hurts. The only way they've been able to gain significance is by drawing attention to their problems. In a small group, they will inevitably plunder everyone's attention and energies, making their needs the centerpiece of meetings.

One young woman I counseled came from a severely dysfunctional home. To get the attention she craved, she created crises; these were the only times her parents would notice her. She developed a drinking problem, then a pattern of dating men who exploited her.

She brought the same pattern into church. Every group she was in sooner or later had to turn its full energies to her. She liked that; she didn't really want her problems solved.

I tried to help her understand the pattern she had gotten stuck in and teach her new behaviors. But it was slow going.

● *I help spawn small groups.* Our primary format for developing small groups is what we call Circles of Concern. For a month, on Tuesday evenings, we meet to discuss a particular problem, with the goal of (1) providing useful information about the problem, and (2) encouraging interaction between those facing the common difficulty.

We designed one Circle of Concern for people making decisions about what to do with elderly parents. On the first Tuesday we scheduled a geriatric worker to talk to the group. The second week the supervisor of four nursing homes in our area discussed the legal and financial factors involved in putting a loved one in such care. The third week I taught a Bible study on how God perceives the aging process and on our need to be sensitive toward the elderly. The final Tuesday, a panel of those who had made these decisions told their experiences and the lessons learned.

The benefits of such strategic and intentional groups continue long afterward. Forty people attended that particular month, and many of them have formed small groups for mutual support. In the Circle of Concern they found common ground.

Some of the other topics covered in Circles of Concern: parents with children who grew up in church but are no longer walking with Christ, singles, financial planning, retirement, long-term illness, specific emotions such as anger, and marriage enrichment (one for those married zero to five years, another for those married five to fifteen years, another for those fifteen years and over).

The key in small groups is to be intentional. We know exactly what we want to accomplish, and we make sure the people know what we're trying to do.

Oversee Worship Attendance

Many years ago some friends referred to me a couple in marital crisis. They had been married ten years, and both were believers. Somehow, though, the husband, a salesman, had maintained a secret lifestyle of drug abuse and adultery. The wife had just discovered it, and when they came into the office, she was angry and bitter.

We began to address the wide range of issues to be dealt with (a process that would take more than a year). But I knew that this, like most problems, was not a problem they could deal with in isolation. They needed the support of the church body and the inspiration and renewal of church worship to stabilize them. At that moment I was again grateful to be a pastor who could oversee their involvement in our church life.

They began attending immediately, which carried them through the initial blowup. Over the next year, I saw the wife weekly, gradually helping her to see how God could restore their relationship. Meanwhile I trained the husband in the discipline of daily Bible study. Over perilous terrain, their marriage was eventually saved, and they have even flourished.

Because people in crisis need all the spiritual input possible, I insist my counselees attend worship. The heart and mind can be healed in public worship in ways that can't happen in my office. In worship, desperate and lonely people can sense the presence and power of God. Such sunshine through the window is especially vital for those who feel distant from God, separated from him by their problems.

Counselees, though, often need a nudge to get to church. A simple "I'll be looking for you on Sunday" helps. With some folks I sweeten the pot by suggesting they meet with my wife and I afterward for lunch (my wife has counseling instincts that go hand in hand with my ministry).

Sometimes I'll introduce them to someone who has weathered similar troubles; attending church with just one friend like that can make the difference between their feeling church is threatening or invitingly familiar. To ease the transition into the relationship, I may have the three of us sit down together. The pastoral counselor can fulfill the vital role of networking better than anyone.

A counselee's involvement in church does present two hurdles. After a couple of sessions together, I usually tell a counselee, "A time will come fairly soon when you'll be sitting in the congregation on Sunday morning and you'll think, *He's preaching at me,* or *He's letting these people know about my problem.* But that won't be the case at all. In the normal course of preaching through Scripture, I unavoidably deal with problems that many people in the congregation have. Be assured I won't put you at risk, and if you think I am, come and talk to me."

I also tell them, "Then the time will come when you're past the crisis, and you'll think, *That man in the pulpit knows more personal things about me than anyone else in the world,* and you'll be uncomfortable with that. You'll feel like packing your bags, moving elsewhere, and starting over. But you should resist that. What I know about you should be the basis for trust and a strong relationship, not for running away."

I also watch for signs of pulling away. If they do, I contact them immediately and try to pull them back in.

I mentioned how the salesman entangled in a secret lifestyle of adultery and drugs began a spiritual discipline of daily Bible study. He became virtually compulsive about it. He credits the Scripture with reshaping his thought patterns and strengthening his will to resist what he could not before. Life-controlling habits don't break easily, but they do fall away when people avail themselves of powerful resources.

Spiritual resources for counseling, though not automatically effective, are supernaturally effective. When used with wisdom, they pierce the very core of a person's being, as Scripture says, "penetrating even to dividing soul and spirit, joints and marrow," healing where other methods cannot touch. I would not want to counsel anyone without them.

When we sit in the counseling room with another person, we represent the church and the good name of Jesus Christ.

— Jim Smith

CHAPTER TWO

Giving Care Ethically

It was a moral and ethical minefield, and Pastor Warren was walking through the middle of it. Every available course seemed rigged for disaster.

Michael Thomas, a prominent school administrator in Pastor Warren's congregation, had been nominated for elder. His election to the board of elders seemed assured, for he was active and well-respected in the church and in community circles. He already sat on the boards of a Christian school system and the metropolitan museum.

But Pastor Warren knew things about Thomas that very few others in the community knew, for Thomas and his wife had come to him for counseling. Pastor Warren knew that this man had a Jekyll-and-Hyde nature. Publicly, he was a learned, respected, socially conscious community leader; privately, he was a destructive, philandering, alcoholic husband. Pastor Warren knew of Thomas' addiction to pornography, sex, alcohol, and psychological abuse of his wife and two children. But his knowledge of Thomas' dark side was covered by the "confidentiality of the confessional."

How could he prevent Thomas from being elected to the church board without breaking faith with the Thomases and with his own conscience as a pastor and counselor? In the nominating committee, Pastor Warren, whose role in which (according to his denomination's polity) is limited to advice, gently tried to propose other names or to suggest that Thomas might be too busy to serve — all to no avail. The Thomas nomination sailed through the committee and was unanimously approved in the congregational meeting. Most troubling of all, because of his background as an educator, he was given responsibility for the children's and youth ministries.

A year and a half later, the church was rocked by scandal when allegations surfaced that Elder Thomas had seduced one woman in the church and made passes at several others. Moreover, he exploded in anger during a youth night program and slapped a female high schooler across the face. Pastor Warren had to persuade the unchurched parents of the student not to sue the church. Thomas resigned from the church board and membership rolls.

The world is becoming increasingly more perilous for churches and pastors. The counseling room, once a safe haven where a pastor could simply counsel and pray with a troubled parishioner for an hour, has become a source of moral anxiety and legal liability. Not all issues are as dramatic as the one just described, but the question of ethics in counseling relationships has never been more important than it is today.

Building and maintaining trust is the key to sustaining ethical relationships with my counselees. When I do things to undermine their trust in me, I'm likely doing something that is or can quickly become unethical. Here, then, are some ways I build trust and thus insure a healthy relationship with the people I counsel.

Building Boundaries

First, I have to build boundaries that will encourage ethical behavior. Here are a couple of broad boundaries I set around my ministry:

● *The appearance of propriety.* For a pastor, the appearance of propriety, being "above reproach," is nearly as important as propriety itself.

I make it a policy in formal counseling situations never to be alone on the premises with the counselee. I don't sit down with a counselee unless someone else — a secretary or a member of the pastoral staff — is close by. On rare occasions when I visit a female counselee in the home, I bring my wife. She may not sit in on the session, but her presence in a nearby room helps guarantee the appearance of propriety.

If someone calls me and asks, "Is my spouse going to you for counseling?" I always answer, "I cannot answer that question, because my counseling schedule is not public information." I give that answer even if the spouse is not coming to see me. Otherwise, that answer would only be a thinly veiled yes.

Sometimes counselees will emotionally attach themselves to counselors in a way that becomes obvious to others outside of the counseling room. Sometimes counselees feel they have acquired a special intimacy with counselors and display inappropriate forms of attention. This kind of behavior needs to be confronted frankly, privately, and as soon as possible.

● *Limited counseling load.* I also limit the number of hours I set aside for formal counseling. The amount of available counseling hours will vary from pastor to pastor and church to church, but I suggest it's not good for a pastor's mental health to devote more than ten hours a week to counseling, unless this is his or her primary responsibility.

The average pastor probably works fifty to sixty hours a week, so that would be about a fifth to a sixth of his or her time, on top of sermon preparation, administration, committee meetings, staff meetings, fixing the copier, stoking the furnace, and whatever else is in the terms of call. I know pastors who get totally overwhelmed by their counseling load because they fail to set limits. They can't get their sermon study done and they rarely see their families. They're so busy trying to fix other people's problems that their own lives are falling apart.

When it comes to working with individuals, I make sure a few other boundaries are in place.

• *Serious counseling is done in the office.* There are times when, in my role as pastor, I'm called to listen to someone's problems, to give a few words of counsel or advice, to offer an encouraging or comforting passage of Scripture. There is an element of counseling when I enter the home of someone who has just lost a loved one or when I meet a church member at a restaurant for lunch. There is even an element of counseling involved when a church member catches me in the hallway and just wants to bend my ear for a minute or two.

But these are not *formal* counseling situations. These are situations where I offer my presence as a pastor and as a friend.

But occasionally I discover that the issues the church member wants to discuss at the funeral home or in the parking lot or on the phone requires more time and a professional setting. At those times I find it helpful to set clear boundaries and ground rules with the counselee.

"I can see that this is a deep and troubling issue for you," I might say. "Could we meet in my office on Tuesday at, say two o'clock?"

Issues I try to keep within the more formal boundaries of the counseling room include premarital counseling, marriage and family counseling, vocational change issues, addiction and compulsive behavior issues, depression and other emotional issues, and deep spiritual and moral issues (such as when a person needs reassurance of God's forgiveness and grace after a major fall).

I've found that there are important practical reasons for structuring a formal counseling session with well-defined boundaries.

Professional boundaries create a different atmosphere for working on issues and problems than the less formal atmosphere of a pastor-parishioner friendship. When in an office setting, there is an agreement to start on time and end on time, the counseling time is spent productively, dealing with real feelings and issues rather than just chatting over generalities.

If the counselee begins to talk around the issue or stray from the subject, I can say, "You know, we have only an hour, and I'd really like to get to the issue." My experience is that when people feel they have unlimited time, they take it. All that does is hinder the counselee's recovery and throw my own schedule into disarray.

● *Time limits are set.* Formal counseling should always require an appointment, and should cover a set length of time, not to exceed an hour. I usually contract initially for eight weekly sessions. If an issue requires more intensive counseling than that, most pastors should refer the counselee to a psychologist, psychiatrist, or psychotherapist.

● *A contract is sometimes used.* In some cases, it may even be helpful to have a written "contract" between counselor and counselee. It doesn't need to be a long document written in legalese, signed, and notarized. It can simply be a memo outlining the times and dates of the counseling appointments and any special expectations, such as, "Mr./Ms. So-and-so will be expected to read such-and-such book, keep a daily journal, and come prepared to discuss his or her insights, feelings, and issues."

These are a few of the boundaries I've put in place, boundaries that in themselves strongly encourage ethical behavior. There are other areas, however, where the boundaries are more intangible. Each counselor must decide how he or she is going to deal with the key ethical dilemmas that arise in counseling. Here's how I come down.

Finances and Gifts

Parishioners like to do nice things for their pastor, and within certain limits they should be able to do so. But when that parishioner is also a counselee, there is an added issue: What if the counselee is giving that gift because of an emotional attachment? Clearly, accepting a gift under such circumstances only promotes that kind of attachment.

I feel the safest course is politely to refuse gifts of any kind from counselees.

For example, a woman I was counseling bought me a very nice necktie. While it may not have been an extravagantly expensive gift, and I had no reason to suspect any motive other than gratitude, I nevertheless had to tell her that, as a matter of professional ethics, I could not accept the tie. When I explained, "Thank you, but gifts have a tendency to confuse or compromise the professional nature of the counseling relationship," she understood and accepted my explanation.

Naturally, there are exceptions. One couple I had once counseled gave me an attractive memento to keep on my desk. It had been about a year since our last counseling session, and I felt we had moved from a counselor-counselee relationship to a pastor-parishioner friendship, so I accepted the gift. Even so, it was a gray area. I always carefully weigh the ethical considerations when I am offered a gift by someone I have counseled.

It also depends on the nature of the gift: expensive or personal gifts such as cash, cologne or shaving lotion, articles of clothing, or jewelry I automatically decline. However, if I clearly see that the gift doesn't transgress other ethical guidelines (like those above) I might accept a less personal gift such as a book or a donation to charity in my name.

And certainly, I will not accept large gifts of cash. In our church, there is a fee charged for pastoral counseling, so people rarely offer me money since they feel they are paying for a service. Still, occasionally someone will say to me, "You've been a real help, Pastor, and I know it's not always easy to make ends meet, so here's five-hundred dollars."

I believe any pastor who accepts that cash is very foolish. Sooner or later, the gift giver is going to come back and start calling markers, because the pastor is now in the giver's debt.

A counselor sometimes has to confront the counselee and say,

"You're way off base. You need to change your thinking and clean up your act." If you are in the counselee's debt, he or she will almost certainly turn that debt against you: "I thought we were friends! How can you talk to me like that after what I've done for you? That's gratitude for you!"

Accepting gifts from a counselee is the rawest form of conflict of interest, and most of the time it should simply be refused.

Confidentiality

A number of years ago I counseled the Flynns, a couple experiencing serious strains in their marriage. Eventually they divorced. Mr. Flynn remarried and a few months later his second wife died under suspicious circumstances. A police detective interviewed me about Mr. Flynn, though no charges were ever filed against him. When answering the detective's questions, I was careful not to disclose confidential information. I simply affirmed information he had gathered from the first wife, information she had given me permission to disclose.

Sometime later, Mr. Flynn became engaged to a third woman, who happened to be a friend of the first wife. The original Mrs. Flynn told the third woman, "You don't know what you're getting into. My ex-husband is dangerous. If you don't believe me, you should at least talk to Pastor Jim Smith." So the third woman called me — and that put me in a difficult ethical and legal position.

I couldn't disclose anything I had learned about Mr. Flynn from our counseling sessions, but I had very good reason to be concerned for this third woman, so I chose my words carefully. "I'm not free to discuss anything I learned in counseling," I told her, "but I would encourage you to be cautious and examine this relationship as objectively as you are able."

Confidentiality is probably the most thorny ethical issue of the pastor-counselee relationship. Confidentiality is crucial in the counseling room, yet it is so easy to trip up and break that trust. I find myself facing the dilemma of confidentiality in at least four ways.

● *Church matters.* Sometimes the ethical requirements of the counselor's role come into direct conflict with the requirements of the pastor's role, as in the story that began this chapter. Pastor Warren knew that Michael Thomas was unfit to serve as an elder, but how could he have conveyed his knowledge to the nominating committee without breaching the confidentiality of his counseling relationship with Thomas?

There are no easy answers, but one tack that some pastors have found effective is to say something like this: "I know Michael Thomas very well, and I'm aware of some issues in his life right now that would make this a bad time for him to be involved in this role. Sometime down the road, perhaps we can put his name in consideration, but at this time it wouldn't be wise to burden him with this responsibility."

There need be no hint as to what those issues are, nor the fact that those issues surfaced during a counseling session. In this approach, any comments regarding Mr. Thomas' fitness of church office should be nebulous, non-specific, and non-judgmental. Someone may ask for more detail, but the pastor should hold his ground and not get drawn into any elaboration beyond the original statement.

If the nomination still went forward, the pastor could talk to Michael Thomas and ask him not to accept. But if Thomas still insisted on being elected to elder, then in my opinion, the pastor would have no choice but to let Thomas be elected. In order to preserve people's long-term trust, we sometimes have to risk such consequences. Admittedly, though, it's a painful choice.

Some would disagree, saying that this is a clear case where the rule of confidentiality must be broken. I respond: unless someone is in imminent danger or the law requires it, confidentiality must be maintained.

As a pastor/counselor, I have essentially three things to offer the counselee: my unconditional acceptance, my trained insight, and an atmosphere of trust. If people can't trust me, I'm out of business. No one will confide in me any longer.

• *Consultations and referrals.* There are some people, though, to whom I must speak about counselees. But I always get the person's permission before doing so. Occasionally I encounter a person whose issues and problems are beyond my abilities and training, so I need to consult with someone else on the pastoral staff or an outside resource person.

So at the beginning of every course of counseling, I ask the counselee to sign a release that gives me permission to consult with other professionals. I also inform the counselee verbally when I need to consult.

"Some of the issues you're dealing with are beyond my training and experience," I'll say. "Would you be willing for me to consult with So-and-so about this issue?" If the person says no, I say, "Well, I have to respect that, but you need to know that we've reached a point beyond which I am unable to help you."

At other times, I may feel the need to refer a person to a support group. So I'll say, "I think you would benefit from being involved in this support group, but they'll want to know some things about you before they allow you into the group. What am I free to share?"

● *Family counseling.* Some of the trickiest aspects of confidentiality arise in family counseling. You have one or two parents and one or more children, each with their own issues — and each deserving of the counselor's confidentiality. But again, even if the situation causes me great anguish, I won't betray a confidence.

If, for example, the pastor is counseling two parents and their teenage son, and the son tells the counselor in confidence, "I'm going to run away from home," I believe the pastor is ethically bound not to reveal this to the parents.

But then, when the boy runs away from home, the parents will probably ask the pastor, "Did he tell you he was planning to do this?" When the pastor admits that he knew, the parents will be understandably angry. "Why didn't you tell us? We could have done something!"

It is small consolation to the parents when the pastor replies, "Because he told me in confidence, and I couldn't betray the confidence."

Or take an even more heart-rending situation: The son tells

the pastor in confidence that he habitually uses dangerous drugs. The wise and conscientious pastor will do everything in his power to obtain the son's permission to tell the parents — but without that permission, the confidence must be kept, even if the counselee is a minor.

● *Inadvertent slips.* I also have to be aware that I can accidentally break a confidence. That's because there is often a fine line between public information and private information.

For example, one of my parishioners, Mrs. Maples, went into the hospital for an operation. The fact that she was in the hospital was public information, and it was announced from the pulpit on Sunday so the congregation could be praying for her. But Mrs. Maples asked that the specific type of surgery she was to undergo be kept confidential. I honored that request for many months — then I let it slip.

Another parishioner, Mrs. Baker, went into the hospital for the same kind of surgery. She was very anxious about her medical condition, and I recalled that Mrs. Maples had shared some things about the surgery that I thought would help ease Mrs. Baker's mind.

"Remember when Mrs. Maples was in the hospital a few months ago?" I said. "Well she had the same procedure you'll be having, and here's what she found out." Only later did I recall that Mrs. Maples had asked me to keep that information confidential.

I immediately called Mrs. Maples and told her what I had done. "I'm so sorry," I said. "This is really embarrassing for me, and I apologize for any embarrassment I've caused you." She was very understanding, and she told me no harm was done. Still, it was a betrayal of privately shared information, which I had no right to share with anyone else.

Few pastors would deliberately break a confidence for the sake of a good sermon illustration, but sometimes we do it inadvertently. I never tell a story that begins, "I once counseled a woman who told me . . . " That's too specific and may cause people to scan the room and wonder who's been talking to me. Instead, I make a generic observation: "People sometimes tell me . . . "

Nor do I tell stories from the pulpit that begin, "Let me tell you about a couple we'll call John and Mary . . ." Such pseudonyms are all too often penetrated by perceptive people (especially in small congregations). What's worse, it makes counselees feel vulnerable and causes them to wonder if they will be next Sunday's sermon illustration.

Also, if I have been counseling Mr. and Mrs. Walters on Thursday afternoon, I don't go out of my way to greet them Sunday morning. If anything, I go out of my way to avoid showing any special attention to people I've been counseling. The fact that people are seeing me as a counselor is a private matter. If I give a church member special attention and someone else infers from that attention that I am seeing that church member professionally, then I have betrayed a confidence.

One final word about confidentiality: the ethics of confidentiality confer great risks and emotional burdens on the counseling pastor. As counselors we carry around in our souls the most explosive and potentially destructive secrets of people's lives. In the vast majority of cases, it is a knowledge we can never reveal under any circumstances. The people who have shared those secrets with us know that we know. And in time, some of those people may begin to resent the fact that we know what we know.

A pastor nurses a parishioner through an emotional crisis, and for a while that parishioner is grateful for the pastor's help and insight. Time passes, and that parishioner turns against the pastor, perhaps even making unfair public accusations against him. The pastor can do nothing but sit and absorb the abuse, knowing the truth and unable to speak it. There is no happy solution to this problem; it's simply an occupational hazard.

Some Legal Considerations

A pastor in North Carolina was sued for alienation of affection because of a sermon he preached.

In my home state of Texas, a pastor was jailed for contempt when he refused to testify regarding matters he was told in confidence in his counseling room.

(In Texas, the only profession covered by privileged communication statutes is the legal profession. If you are a professional counselor in Texas, you learn to keep your notes so garbled and coded that no outsider can make sense of them even if they are subpoenaed.)

The pastoral calling exposes one to all manner of legal liabilities. Three areas we must be aware of are:

● *Legal limits to confidentiality.* There are three issues that people occasionally bring into the counseling room which ethically and legally transcend a counselor's commitment to confidentiality. As counselors we are required to disclose rather than conceal these issues because they involve acts or potential acts of violence. These issues are:

1. Child abuse

2. Contemplation of suicide

3. Contemplation of homicide

Child abuse should be reported to the appropriate social agency (the name of that social agency varies from place to place but is usually a county agency with a name such as Child Protective Services).

If a person acts suicidal, the counselor should try to get the person to agree verbally or in writing that he or she will not commit suicide before seeing the counselor again. If the person will not agree, then the counselor needs to take the person to a county hospital, or call the police to do so.

If a person threatens the life of another in counseling, the counselor is ethically bound to tell the person who has been threatened. In our church, when a counselor makes such a call, we always make sure the call is witnessed by another staff member; a memo is then written and signed by counselor and the witness.

No matter the circumstance and course of action the counselor takes, it is highly recommended afterward to write a memo outlining the time, date, and nature of the incident and what the counselor did as a result.

The demands of the law on the pastor-counselor are very

stringent. In California, a church was sued (albeit unsuccessfully) when a counselor failed to report the suicidal intentions of a counselee. Moreover, a counselor who learns of an incident of child abuse and fails to report it will not merely be sued; he or she may be prosecuted.

• *Giving testimony.* Another hazard to approach carefully in the pastor's role is testifying in a court trial. It is not unusual for a pastor to be thrust into the middle of other people's court battles. I have personally been subpoenaed several times to testify or give depositions in child custody cases because of my counseling relationship with the parents.

In such cases, I decline to testify unless I get a written release from the parents. In most cases, both parents have given me the release in the apparent belief I would give them each a "good rap." But if I just get a release from one parent, I only testify regarding the person who has given me the release.

For example, Mrs. Jones has given me a written release to disclose our counseling conversations but Mr. Jones has not. If I am asked, "Did Mr. Jones beat his wife?" I will answer, "Mrs. Jones reported to me that he beat her." Even if Mr. Jones admitted to me that he beat her, I can't disclose that fact because it is covered by confidentiality, and Mr. Jones has not given me permission to disclose it.

• *Lawsuits.* A pastor would expect (and deserve) to be sued if he became sexually involved with a counselee or manipulated the counselee for financial gain. But a pastor can also be sued for malpractice if he attempts to give counsel in an area where he has no expertise.

The fact is, anyone can sue anyone for anything. Even if the person suing you loses, the cost of defending yourself can be catastrophically expensive. That's why it's important to have a sufficient amount of liability insurance in place.

I've been told that in today's litigious climate, a million dollars of liability coverage is the bare minimum any counselor should carry, regardless of his or her profession. One can debate the figures, but personal liability coverage does not usually protect us if we were to be sued in our professional capacity, so we are wise to make sure that some form of professional liability policy is in place.

Intervention: Walking into a Buzz Saw

The word *intervention* is becoming increasingly popular in our culture, and pastors are frequently asked to step into the middle of volatile domestic problems: "Pastor, my husband is drunk and violent! Please come now!" Or, "Pastor, I just found out my wife is having an affair. Would you come over and help me confront her about it?" Or, "Pastor, my teenage son is using cocaine. Please come talk to him!"

However, I've never found that type of intervention to be helpful. So I don't do it.

If people are in pain and willing to work on their pain, they will come into my office, and we can work together in that structured environment. But if one party to the problem is not motivated to work on the problem, the pastor who seeks to intervene is just walking into a buzz saw.

There is a good reason why police officers hate to get involved in domestic situations: they are often extremely dangerous (even deadly) situations. I'm not eager to jump into a situation that would give a heavily armed police officer pause. I never know what I may walk into — and I've only heard one person's version of the story.

I try to find alternatives to intervention. If I'm counseling a woman, for example, and she asks me to talk to her husband, I may call him and ask him to come to my office. "Your wife is counseling with me," I'll say, "and it would be easier for me to help her if I could have some time with you to get your insights." If I make contact with the husband in a way that is non-judgmental and non-threatening, and if I refer to the wife as the patient, he's more likely to come in and talk. But if he flatly refuses, I will not try to force my way into the situation.

I strongly believe that a counselor does not belong in the middle of people's problems and issues. A counselor is an outside source of insight, perspective, and encouragement. As soon as a counselor becomes entangled, directly or indirectly, in the problems of the counselee, that counselor is bound to run afoul of the ethical and legal boundaries of his profession.

A Fragile Trust

Ironically, the best defense against failing ethically in counseling is to remind myself daily that I am a fallible human being, with the same capacity for self-deception and hidden motivation as those who come to me for counseling. That realization forces me to continually check myself to insure that there is no hint of exploitation of any counselee, male or female, for any reason — emotional, financial, or ego related.

I also try to remember the trust that's been handed to me, and how fragile that trust is.

I recently heard the story of a troubled young woman named Janet who at age 14 was seduced by a church counselor. The relationship has continued off and on through the years, so that now, at the age of 32, Janet continues to be emotionally enmeshed with this man, who has long since left the ministry. The relationship has been enormously painful for Janet and continues to set back her emotional recovery.

Rev. Edwards, senior pastor of the church where this ex-counselor once worked, has met with Janet several times in his counseling room. Representing the church to her, he has asked her forgiveness for what this man did to her. Some healing has taken place in her life, but it's a toss up whether she will ever be strong enough to sever her emotional ties to this destructive man.

When we sit in the counseling room with another person, we represent the church and the good name of Jesus Christ. When we exploit the vulnerability of the hurting person under our care, the pain and destruction that results is incalculable and long lasting.

Then again, when we act in the manner of our Lord, as people who can be trusted, we are entrusted with bearing others' burdens and seeing people experience liberation from spiritual and emotional bondage. And that makes the risks and burdens of counseling more than worthwhile.

People usually see a professional counselor for psychological relief. People often go to a pastor for spiritual relief. This puts the pastoral counselor in not only a healing role but also a discipling role.
— Gary Gulbranson

CHAPTER THREE

The Preaching Ingredient

My wife's father and mother used to attend our church. One Sunday night, as she had done many times before, my mother-in-law played piano in the service. Two days later she collapsed and was taken to the hospital, where the doctors determined she had a brain aneurysm. On Friday she died.

Although grieving with my family and congregation, I decided to preach on Sunday. My sermon, from the Book of Joshua, discussed the sovereignty of God. I related the message to her death and spoke openly about my own feelings.

Later in the foyer, I overheard a woman from the church say, "Well at least now Pastor Gulbranson knows a little about the pain some of us have gone through." At the moment I thought it was a cruel statement.

Later I thought about her comment. It was, in fact, a perception of me shared by a few others. Because of the standards I preached, some regarded me as lacking empathy.

Yet I shouldered a heavy load of counseling and relied heavily on my training in listening skills and empathy. I prayed for my counselees and took their problems home at night. Of those who came to me for counseling, I doubt if any would label me as critical or unaccepting.

It seemed, at least in the eyes of some, that Pastor Gulbranson in the office and Preacher Gulbranson in the pulpit had little to do with one another. And that perception undercut some of my effectiveness as their minister.

As a result of that experience, I began consciously to let my counseling strengths find greater expression in the pulpit. It has made a marked difference.

In turn, my style of counseling has also evolved over the years, due partly to what I know about preaching, making me, I think, a much more effective counselor.

Just as all-around gymnasts perform better on rings because of the flexibility they develop on floor exercise, and better on floor exercise because of the strength they develop on rings, so pastors can be more effective overall because of the mutually beneficial ministries of preaching and counseling.

As I learned in the experience above, however, the synergy of preaching and counseling is not automatic. Here's how I make the most of it.

How Counseling Shapes My Preaching

There's an old saying that a preacher should prepare sermons with the Bible in one hand and the newspaper in the other, meaning that our exegesis ought to touch the daily lives of our people. More helpful than the newspaper is counseling. In fact, I've found that counseling helps my preaching in at least four ways.

● *Counseling helps me select topics.* During my first few years at Glen Ellyn Bible Church, a lot of new people began attending. For many this was their first church experience; others hadn't been to church since childhood. With them they brought all kinds of struggles, especially family problems, emotional hurts, and an inability to forgive. Some had a hard time grabbing hold of God's forgiveness and reordering their lives.

I counseled most of these people in my office, indeed suffered with them, anxious about their turmoils. One day I happened upon a book of the Bible that spoke to a common thread of their experience — Hosea. God had asked Hosea to live in a wrenching situation in order to communicate who God is. He was a God who had been betrayed, who had been hurt, yet who still passionately loved his people.

So for several months, I preached from Hosea, and we saw lives healed and hope restored. That sermon series, which impacted people as much as any other sermon series I've preached, germinated in the counseling office as I listened to people and saw the circumstances of life up close.

Counseling compels me to preach to people's needs. Marriages on the rocks, confused youth, questions about God's will, bitterness — as I brush up against real life each day, the answers in God's Word often beg to be preached to the entire congregation.

● *Counseling helps me identify the emotions of a text.* For me, identifying and communicating the emotional texture of a passage is what distinguishes preaching from teaching. The text is not just ethereal ideas, impersonal principles, and detached theology, but people — commands for people, sins of people, dilemmas of people. The sons and daughters of Adam and Eve are beset with complexity and pain, joys and hope — an emotional smorgasbord.

My sermon preparation and delivery is intensely personal. I often have the faces of counselees in mind as I prepare messages. Not that I preach at those individuals, but their lives, being significant to me, make the truth of Scripture ring with emotion. Also, as I preach, the faces in the sanctuary stimulate unanticipated thoughts and emotions in me.

This helps me project the Word not just to the head but also to the heart.

• *Counseling helps me ask the empathy question.* I often ask myself during my sermon preparation, *How will the person going through this situation or being corrected by this verse or falling short of this ideal feel about what I am saying?* Whether their feelings are right or wrong is not the issue; what matters is how I can help them through those feelings to move in the direction of God's will. My answering the empathy question enables the listener to hear not only the letter of the Word but the spirit of the Word.

In one sermon series, "I Believe in the God Who Believes in Me," based on the Gospel of John, I dealt with the subject of self-image by looking at the interactions of Jesus with Nicodemus, with the woman at the well, and with others. At the same time I was counseling a young woman who had grown up in a dysfunctional home. Her father had left when she was a little girl; several male figures had come and gone, abusing her in the process. After a string of negative dating experiences, she eventually married and later came to know Christ. But she still had curdled ideas about her identity and life in general.

As I prepared my sermons each week, my mind would frequently turn to her. When I preached about John, the disciple whom Jesus loved, I emphasized John's special ability to notice the love Christ uniquely had for him. The following week this woman came to my office for her appointment and said the message had been transforming. Even though we had discussed many of the same ideas before, hearing them in a sermon affected her differently. I think our discussions helped me to ask better the empathy question and focus that sermon in a way that would address her emotions.

The empathy question impacts the application section of my sermons. This is especially important when I'm preaching about sins like child or wife abuse, because my temptation is to get angry and blast people with generalities. Neither the blast nor the generalities are much help.

Instead, I put myself in the place of the people hearing my message and ask, "How are they going to hear what I'm saying?" Dealing with their feelings, then, becomes the first step in application, for a person's feelings skew everything else they try to do.

In addition, when I've thought about how people are going to react, I think more realistically and specifically about what they probably will and will not do after the service. In short, I try to understand the pain of those who will be bloodied by the sharp "two-edged sword" of Scripture.

In that sense, I've been given a glimpse of the Old Testament prophets. They were not smug and self-righteous, not Pharisees who gloated over the judgments to come. They spoke clearly about right and wrong — and wept in the process, anticipating the feelings, thoughts, and responses of people.

● *Counseling is a source of illustrations.* Obviously this requires sensitivity and careful attention to safeguards. Past or present counselees listening to a sermon naturally tend to read themselves into any illustrations or comments I make, especially if they are emotionally on edge or their self-image is teetering. But with conscientious protection of confidences, counseling becomes an artist's palette for coloring my sermons.

There are three primary safeguards.

1. I illustrate more with generic circumstances dealt with on numerous occasions than with an individual's story. For example, "I talk with many wives who can't get in spiritual sync with their husbands. They feel lonely at home and frustrated when they come to church. 'He just doesn't show interest in what is happening between me and the Lord,' is the common complaint." A generic illustration isn't as gripping, but it still helps people hear and see the relevance of Scripture.

2. If I tell someone's story, I request permission. To avoid surprises or misunderstandings, I inform the person in detail what I would like to say and the context in which it will be told in the sermon. Most people are grateful that their painful circumstances can help others. Although we often discuss how I can keep their identity hidden, rarely has anyone refused me permission.

3. I will use stories from my past, before I came to Glen Ellyn. I make sure listeners know they don't know the person in the story. I also tell it in such a way that it doesn't dishonor the person in the story. I don't want anyone in my congregation to think, *I would never want a preacher telling a story about me in this way.*

How My Preaching Influences Counseling

If people's lives need to get into the sermon, the Word of God, written and spoken, needs to get into the counseling session. Being a preacher has enabled me do that, helping me deepen and improve my counseling ministry.

● *Preaching provokes listeners to come to counseling who might not otherwise come.* Often sermons stir listeners' interest in something, opening their eyes to what they perhaps had grown complacent about. It reveals needs they have suppressed or ignored or simply endured but now want to resolve.

People come to preachers for counseling for different reasons than they go to full-time counselors. People usually see a professional counselor for psychological relief. People often go to a pastor for spiritual relief. They come seeking guidance in decision making as well as specific application of the Scriptures in their lives. This puts the pastoral counselor in not only a healing role but also a discipling role, and the basis for counseling becomes the Scriptures and their meaning.

In addition, as I give people glimpses into my personal life when I preach, many are prompted to come for counseling; they can identify with me.

I've been extensively involved with the business world. While pursuing my doctorate, I worked for almost eight years in real estate investment. I am on the board of a bank and interact regularly with business people through the Rotary club. As a result, my sermon applications and illustrations are often business related. After such sermons, I am often approached for counseling by business people who now see me as more credible.

● *People who hear me preach expect answers in counseling.* Those who come to pastors want more than empathy and affirmation, which I give; primarily they come to a pastor/preacher to learn what God's Word says about their situation. They sense in preaching a source of wisdom and authority they can't find outside of Scripture. They come to me because they rightly assume that the source of truth in preaching and counseling is the same.

Over the years I've become increasingly directive in my counseling. I'm more willing to point people to what's right and wrong, as you might expect more of a preacher than a counselor. Many people in our day live with deep insecurities. They crave a moral, ordered world. Especially in light of so much moral confusion, I want to be as clear as possible about morality, even if it troubles them at first.

One pastor I know had a single woman come to see him. She had been sleeping with a man occasionally. She complained, "Whenever I give myself to him, he loses interest in me for a couple of weeks. Then he starts paying attention to me until we sleep together again." She couldn't figure out what was going on.

My friend gently but firmly explained the biblical counsel about extra-marital sex and outlined its wisdom. Her response: "This is a new age. You can't live like that anymore." She left the office clearly disturbed, but with an understanding of what God's answer was to her situation. She didn't like God's answer, but she wasn't finding the world's alternative any more satisfying.

Like that pastor, I explain what's right and wrong, but I also urge people, when appropriate, to do what's right. I make it clear that it's their choice, but I let them know what I hope they will do. When counseling in a directive manner, of course, appropriateness is everything. The owner of a trucking business attended my church years ago, and he unloaded some wisdom on a young preacher. "You can't drive a 12-ton truck over a 10-ton bridge."

I had been trying to, but with little success. I would rev my engines and roll an eighteen wheeler of God's will onto people, and they would collapse; they wouldn't come back to church or to counseling.

Jesus criticized the Pharisees for the same thing, for laying heavy burdens upon people without lifting a finger to help them.

My mistake was I had not yet established enough trust in our relationship or built enough faith in God or encouraged them sufficiently with God's love and good news. So I have learned to first build bridges both in preaching and counseling.

● *Listeners come for unique, personal application of sermon principles.* As true as scriptural principles are in general, they often require application to an individual's unique needs, problems, weaknesses, and gifts.

One woman attended our church sporadically because of agoraphobia, the fear of public places. On one Sunday when she was present, my sermon included the statement: "It is God's will for you regularly to attend church."

She called that week and came in for counseling. "You don't know what it's like to suffer with this fear," she said. "Sometimes I will have panic attacks while in church: I can't breathe; my heart starts racing; I break out in a sweat; I feel like I'm going to lose my mind. God doesn't want me to suffer like that. How can I come to church when I suspect this is going to happen?"

As often happens, she had a problem but saw few options. I showed her how to defuse some of the threat. "God wants to help you overcome this, and church is one of the easiest places to do that. You can sit in the balcony if you want. You can come a little late and leave quickly so that you don't have to interact with a lot of people. We are a large church, so you can remain fairly anonymous until you become more comfortable. It will be hard at first, but eventually if you take these first steps, things will get better, and you'll be able to go out to other public places."

The personal integration made the difference, and it was the very thing she hoped counseling would do for her. Counseling helped her see how she, with her barriers, could obey God. She started attending every Sunday and eventually got a job in a Christian organization.

Not every case is this easy, however. Sometimes people come wanting personal application but then object when I give it. They want to hold the truth at arm's length. They avoid it intentionally. At such times I get specific about the actions they need to take.

• *Since I preach for decision, I can counsel for decision.* Each week after my sermons I use a variety of invitations to challenge people to respond to the message. Since people are used to that from the pulpit, they are not surprised when I use that same approach in the counseling setting. So I lay out the options, explain God's will, urge them to do what's right, and then tell them they have a decision to make. I can't make it for them.

Most people in counseling feel like victims, as though they're trapped. They feel they don't have any options or decisions available: the problem is a result of their past, other people, or unchangeable circumstances, and they are left with no apparent control of their lives.

So after talking through their problems, I tell people, "We've talked about your past, but that's not an excuse for your present; it's an explanation. This is how God sees your difficulty. We need to focus on what your choices are today."

Most of the time, I'm confident people will decide for the right, but even when I'm not, I still want to bring them to a point of decision.

One woman who came to me with marital difficulties was extremely withdrawn, shy, and noncommunicative. For three sessions I gradually drew her out, patiently listening to bits and pieces about how terrible her husband was, how he never met her needs, how frustrated she was, and what a victim she was.

Finally, in the fourth session the truth came out: she had been entangled in an adulterous relationship for years. Having made a commitment to Christ, though not actively attending church, she was carrying a heavy load of guilt.

We talked about God's will. I laid out her options and the consequences. "You can continue in this other situation," I said, "be miserable, and feel tugged and torn. Or you can leave your husband, go off and marry this guy, and grab a measure of happiness for yourself, but more than likely you will be frustrated; there will be brokenness that won't disappear. Or you can ask God's forgiveness; you can turn around and start moving in the right direction. We'll work with you and your husband to restore what has been broken."

She exercised her freedom. She never came back to see me, and she chose to leave her husband. I've lost touch and have no idea what has happened since.

Though it usually doesn't turn out so bad, that's still a painful thing for a counselor to experience. But it's unavoidable.

Several years ago my mother wrote a Christmas letter in which she said, "This has been the toughest year of my life." All of her kids, she said, were grown, but some had made bad decisions and were suffering terribly. She felt guilty about their problems, nagged by the idea that if she had "been a better mother" or had come to Christ sooner, some of these things wouldn't have happened.

Then God gave her an insight. Though he was a perfect parent, his first two children chose wrong. She wrote, "If God, the perfect parent, was not going to control the choices of his children, I realized I needed to exercise that same attitude toward my children."

I have learned the same lesson about my counselees.

The Goal of Both: Applying God's Truth

I grew up in a home with many problems, problems in my parent's marriage, struggles between parents and children. When my folks came to know the Lord (I was 11 at the time), they were extremely fortunate to have a pastor who got close to them and demonstrated real care.

During the week he would take the truth presented on Sunday morning and explain to my parents, who lacked some basic living skills, how to integrate the biblical truths with their situation. Otherwise it would have been an extremely frustrating and discouraging experience to sit for long under his preaching.

Because a preacher got close enough to understand what was going on and help us through the struggles, we made it.

I can't imagine my preaching apart from being involved with people in counseling. To get close and wrestle with the human condition and to explore the depths of God's Word, to speak to people's situations from the pulpit and in the counseling setting —

these are to me the perfect, indispensable complements of pastoral
ministry.

When diagnosing a problem, we must first try to find the most obvious and natural explanation before moving on to explain it in more complex or less obvious ways.
— *Archibald Hart*

Regeneration, Deliverance, or Therapy?

Pastor Jones was perplexed. For the fourth time in a month Cynthia, a 24-year-old, single woman, had come to see him, each visit more puzzling than the last.

Cynthia had grown up in his church, where her parents were long-standing members. Cynthia had professed faith at a youth meeting when she was 14 and had been a leader in the youth group before going away to college. Now she was home again, looking for a job.

At her first session with Pastor Jones, Cynthia explained that two years earlier she had started dating a young man. They became serious but fought often and frequently broke up.

"A year ago, I discovered I was pregnant," she finally said. "And against my better judgment, I had an abortion."

Troubled by both the relationship and the abortion, she felt "locked in," unable to extricate herself from either the relationship or her past behavior.

"What can I do?" she wailed. "Where can I go to get away from all of this? What's wrong with me that I can't break off this sick relationship?"

Pastor Jones listened with deep sympathy to Cynthia. He reasoned with her and then prayed for her. She felt better.

But a few days later she was back again. He listened to her repeat her anxieties and guilt. *She seems worse, maybe even depressed,* Pastor Jones thought. *Why isn't she experiencing forgiveness and freedom? Has she really experienced conversion? Is perhaps some demonic power at work in her?*

Not that he had had much experience in spiritual warfare, but so many groups were talking about it he couldn't help but consider it.

Still, he repeated his standard counseling format: he helped her confess her sins and pray for forgiveness. Then he hoped God would work a miracle.

Twice more she came back, even more troubled still. Pastor Jones was baffled and even a little irritated. *Could it be,* he wondered, *she has some deep-seated emotional problem? Has something snapped in her mind, or is there something bad from her childhood coming back to haunt her?*

He felt inadequate. But he hesitated to refer her to someone else for fear Cynthia and others would think him incompetent. This seemed a spiritual problem. Why couldn't he just do his job as a pastor? He stewed about what to do.

Pastor Jones is not alone here. I have heard this story, with minor variations, over and over from pastors. No pastor can become an expert in every aspect of the human condition. There isn't enough time in one life to master everything a pastor should know about ministry or about counseling.

And yet every pastor has to diagnose, if only at a rudimentary level, a troubled person's problem: Does this person need to be pointed toward making a commitment to Christ and thereby experience the new life of regeneration? Does this person need some supernatural intervention? Or is this a case for psychotherapy or counseling?

Before I set out some guidelines for diagnosing people who come to see pastors, first let me discuss two factors that complicate a diagnosis: (1) how psychological factors, especially childhood experiences, can impact or impede spiritual healing; (2) the difference between demon possession and its most popular imitator, schizophrenia.

Psychological Scars

Hardly anyone reaches adulthood without collecting a few psychological scars on the way. Even Christian homes can be severely dysfunctional and anxiety producing. Abuse can take many forms. The worst is not physical but emotional.

Divorce is increasingly common even in Christian circles, wreaking havoc on the social and emotional lives of children. Or psychological damage can be caused by bad parenting — neglectful, overly permissive, or overly repressive.

In later life these scars can interfere with a person's spiritual development and prevent a free, unhindered experience of Christ.

For example, our understanding of God is very much shaped by childhood experiences of people significant to us. When a father, for instance, is abusive, demanding, cold, or unforgiving, we are likely to assume that most authority figures, even God, are that way.

One woman told me, "I can't approach God without confusing him with my father. I can't pray with my eyes closed because if I do, I see images of my father towering over me and making threats. I can't even pray the Lord's Prayer, because saying 'Our Father' sends fears flashing through my body. God and my father seem to be the same — emotionally I can't tell the difference. When someone speaks of God's love, I haven't the slightest idea what they're talking about. It's all very confusing to me."

This woman will have great difficulty in developing a healthy and balanced spiritual life. Scores of people in most churches suffer from such distorted images of God. When such people are in emotional pain, these distortions will hinder their ability to appropriate God's help.

A pastor counseling such a person will need much wisdom in correcting these distortions. Merely educating people in the "attributes of God," teaching them about who God really is, is only part of the counseling task.

The psychological damage needs to be healed, and while God does sometimes intervene in wonderful ways to erase these scars, other times such supernatural intervention does not occur. (God does not always short-circuit the healing process partly, I believe, because in the long run we are better persons when we "work through" these problems by God's grace, rather than experiencing instantaneous cures.)

False guilt is another example of psychological damage that can hinder spiritual growth. Many children raised in devout Christian homes are traumatized by excessive and unrelenting guilt. Sometimes parents, yearning to raise "God-fearing" children, impose rigid discipline and practice severe punishment.

For instance, one Christian family, who lived in a house next to us when we first arrived in the United States, had strict rules about whom their three daughters could talk to. The parents were so scared that their girls would become "contaminated by the world," they told them, "You may not have any conversation with a non-Christian child. If we catch you talking to such a person, we will punish you."

These children developed intense guilt about talking to non-Christians. My daughters (who were allowed to be their friends) would listen for hours to their fears. Our neighbor's daughters grew up to be excessively guilt ridden; one now suffers from a major emotional disorder.

This sort of guilt is often referred to as neurotic or false guilt, as opposed to true or healthy guilt. Although many psychologists see all guilt as false, I do not. We need healthy guilt. We need to develop a clear sense of right or wrong. But when we feel condemned by arbitrary rules, or when the guilt we feel far excedes what is appropriate, then it becomes neurotic.

Why is it neurotic? For one important reason: such guilt does not respond to forgiveness, whether it is offered by human beings or God. It only knows punishment. It demands to be punished. It won't let up even when all is fully restored.

This was the problem with Cynthia (the person Pastor Jones was counseling). Her upbringing made her conscience oversensitive and out of control. She could find no way out of the prison of guilt brought on by her wayward behavior. Having strayed, she could not find her way back to the peace of mind that forgiveness from God should have provided.

Is this purely a spiritual problem? Obviously not. Can God not miraculously cure such a problem? Yes, but often he doesn't. God's wisdom is far greater than ours, and his concern is much more for our sanctification than our comfort. Cynthia needed to replace her neurotic guilt with a healthy sense of guilt. She also needed to experience forgiveness — the deep and profound forgiveness that God offers her, conditional upon her repentance — so that she could come to live with her imperfections.

Schizophrenia and Demon Possession

If psychological trauma, especially in childhood, can impede spiritual growth, what about spiritual powers? How do these impact psychological or spiritual problems?

I encounter scores of emotionally troubled people every year who at one time or another have been told they have an evil spirit or a demon possessing them. But demon possession is not always the problem.

Not every person who has a sexual addiction is under the control of a "lust demon." Lustful thoughts and behavior can be the consequence of poor self-control, inappropriate exposure to sexual activity as a child, sexual abuse, or ordinary sin. We don't need to jump to exotic explanations.

In addition, it can be harmful to assume demon possession too readily. No doubt Satan appreciates the extra publicity, but even worse, the hopelessness that such a label, especially when untrue, engenders in the victim (especially after exorcisms fail to cure the problem) can often do more harm than the original problem.

Falsely attributing emotional problems to demons has several dangers: It removes the victim from responsibility for recognizing and confessing *human* sinfulness. It enhances Satan's power inappropriately. But most importantly, it delays the introduction of effective treatment.

And delaying treatment for a problem like schizophrenia can significantly decrease the likelihood of the sufferer's return to normality.

Schizophrenia is a physical disease. Because it exhibits bizarre symptoms, it is frequently labeled as demon possession. But just as we learned with epilepsy (another disease formerly labeled as demon possession), we now know that schizophrenia is the result of a defect in brain chemistry. Medication can cure people of it.

And any delay in starting the right medication for treating schizophrenia can impact the sufferer's long-term recovery. Misdiagnosis here can have serious consequences. This is especially true for a form of schizophrenia that starts in late adolescence.

Every pastor, therefore, should be able to recognize the basic symptoms of schizophrenia. Frankly, those who cannot should not be counseling. Some basic symptoms include:

● Marked social isolation or withdrawal;

● Marked inability to function as wage-earner, student, or homemaker;

● Markedly peculiar behavior (e.g., collecting garbage, talking to self in public, hoarding food);

● Marked impairment in personal hygiene and grooming;

● Digressive, vague, over-elaborate conversation, or lack of conversation, or lack of content in conversation;

- Odd beliefs or magical thinking that affect the person's behavior (e.g., superstitiousness, belief in clairvoyance, telepathy, "others can feel my feelings");

- Unusual experiences (e.g., recurrent illusions, sensing the presence of a force or person not actually present);

- Marked lack of initiative or energy.

Schizophrenia is a complex disease, and if a pastor suspects it in a client, he or she should make the appropriate referral as quickly as possible.

If this is schizophrenia, though, what does demon possession look like? The characteristics of demon possession are not neat and simple to discern, but those with extensive experience with possession look for such things as:

- *The presentation of a new personality.* The person's voice and expressions change, and he or she begins acting and speaking like a different person. However, this is also seen in "multiple personality disorders," a severe psychological problem associated with "splitting" and childhood abuse. It takes someone trained in psychopathology to tell the difference.

- *A striking lack of human warmth.* The possessed seem barren and empty, and they lack empathy.

- *Marked revulsion to Christian symbols.* The cross, Bible, and other Christian symbols make the possessed extremely uncomfortable. However, I also see many schizophrenics evidence this reaction. So this sign, by itself, is not evidence of possession.

- *Physical phenomena.* Many describe an inexplicable stench, freezing temperatures, flying objects and a "smooth, stretched skin" (see Malachi Martin's *Hostage to the Devil*).

- *Behavioral transformations.* The victim has "possessed gravity," in other words, cannot be moved physically or can levitate or float.

Obviously, then, possession is not as common as is supposed, and many so-called possessions have more natural explanations. Diagnosis of demon possession is usually a matter of eliminating the obvious causes of the problem first.

How should the pastoral counselor set about making a diagnosis of possession? By ensuring that other professionals also examine the person to be certain that no obvious cause of the problem is being overlooked. If all natural explanations are exhausted and several of the above symptoms are present, then the pastor may wish to proceed with such a diagnosis.

The Law of Parsimony

In all matters of discernment the principle that should guide us is the "law of parsimony."

In essence, this law requires that we try to understand a problem at its most obvious and fundamental level. Simplicity is the rule. When diagnosing a problem, we must *first* try to find the most obvious and natural explanation *before* moving on to explain it in more complex or less obvious ways.

For instance, if I have a headache, I first try to see it as a result of stress or eyestrain (depending on the circumstances). If rest doesn't cure it, I may then need to consider whether I have a bad case of the flu. If that hypothesis doesn't pan out, I may need to go to a neurologist to check if I have a brain tumor.

But unless the symptoms obviously suggest a brain tumor, I don't immediately jump to the conclusion that every time my head hurts I have a tumor. All diagnostic processes follow this law.

Here's how we can apply that law to the pastoral counselor's task of determining the nature of a person's problem.

1. Take a careful history. This lesson we can borrow from other disciplines like medicine. Most pastors are not trained to take a thorough history, but it is vitally important if you are not going to miss an obvious cause of a problem. A history should include the following:

— Details of family background.

— History of dysfunctional patterns in the family.

— History of mental illness in the family.

— History of the presenting problem.

— When it first occurred.

— How often it occurs.

— The changes that have taken place in recent history.

— History of spiritual experience and practice.

— Experience of conversion — when, where, and how?

— Patterns of spiritual development since conversion.

A thorough history should provide a clear picture of what troubles the person, how it started, and the context of the problem.

2. Consider obvious causes first. Following the law of parsimony, you now try to explain the problem in the most obvious or natural terms.

For instance, if there is a history of mental illness in the family and the person you are counseling is experiencing bizarre behavior or emotions, the most likely cause is the familial pattern of illness. Genetic factors strongly influence the severe mental disorders. Unless you are trained in psychopathology, however, the most responsible action you can take is to refer the troubled person to a psychologist or psychiatrist for diagnosis.

3. Intervene at the most obvious level first. It is helpful to think of counseling intervention in hierarchical terms. Not only does diagnosis work upwards from the obvious level of explanation, many interventions should also follow this approach. Treat the basic symptoms first, then move on to more complex symptoms.

For instance, a man may be behaving bizarrely and saying he sees things or hears voices that no one else sees or hears. The first intervention should be to refer the man to a competent professional who will treat these unusual behaviors and hallucinations.

While treatment for the bizarre behavior is under way you may wish to counsel the person in the steps of Christian commitment, encouraging a surrender to the claims of Christ. (Your responsibility as pastor doesn't end when you make a referral.) Of course, the one intervention (professional treatment) may need temporarily to take precedence over the other (spiritual guidance) simply because the disease needs to be under control before the person can adequately comprehend spiritual matters.

4. *Consider supernatural causes.* At what point should one consider the possibility of supernatural or demonic causes for a problem and invoke deliverance as the remedy? Only when the more obvious causes have been eliminated.

If there is a history of schizophrenia in the immediate family of a troubled person, for instance, the treatment of schizophrenia must be given first consideration. I think it is gross negligence to move beyond this diagnosis without addressing the presenting issue.

But what about less bizarre behaviors? The same principle applies. Find the most obvious cause and treat this first. If you have eliminated the obvious, or if the symptoms are so strange as to rule out any natural cause, then you might want to consider moving directly to supernatural factors.

Some words of caution:

● Never try to diagnose supernatural causes by yourself. Always seek corroboration from others, and hold yourself accountable to the corporate discernment.

● Remember that many experts believe that possession doesn't usually manifest itself in bizarre behavior. Satan is more creative than that. We may need to look elsewhere for it.

● Even when you think there is a state of possession, remember that psychological or psychosomatic problems accompany and complicate possession. These may *also* need treatment.

● While Jesus instructed his followers to deal with demons (Luke 9:1-2), we find no injunction to seek them out. In other words, avoid preoccupation with these causes. Focus rather on the victory and protection we have in Christ.

5. *Consider the need for regeneration.* One of the great drawbacks of counseling or psychotherapy is that it does not deal directly with the core problem of human existence: our alienation from God.

Whatever the problem that a troubled parishioner presents, the question of regeneration is always a legitimate one. Without the regeneration that God works in the core of our being, all human endeavor to improve the quality of life (mental or physical) is limited. Pastoral diagnosis must always address the question of whether or not regeneration has occurred.

I am not saying that we judge people's salvation. But we have a right to call people to accountability for their souls. This is the work of evangelism.

During emotional turmoil people are more open to spiritual interventions. The caring pastor will carefully suggest ways the client can experience renewal by receiving God's grace. *Regeneration* literally means "rebirth," and only when the core (or "heart") is regenerated can counseling or psychotherapy make a significant difference.

As Christian counselors we can prepare a person to be receptive to God's work. We can help remove the obstacles of childhood traumas or distorted God images so that God's grace can be effective. Therapy or counseling does not do the work of grace; it merely aids it. It is nothing more than burden bearing as instructed by Galatians 6:2 and Romans 15:1, helping others to rely upon the greatest burden bearer of all (Mt. 8:17).

6. Don't delay in referring. Whenever a problem is complicated or when you feel that it is beyond your training or expertise, refer the person to someone capable. Develop a relationship with a group of trusted professionals to whom you can make referrals.

Let me emphasize the word *trust.* Unless you know these professionals personally you will not have complete trust in them. Cultivate a relationship with them. Go to lunch and talk to them so that they understand where you come from. Find out their orientation. If you are not satisfied, move on to someone else.

And even after you've made your referral, maintain ongoing contact so that you can evaluate progress and decide when and how you will intervene with spiritual direction.

While I suggest a parsimonious model of diagnosis, I cannot stress too strongly the importance of continuing education for pastors, especially in the area of understanding the human condition. Ignorance here is dangerous and can do much harm.

The misapplication of a spiritual solution may delay appropriate treatment of serious mental disorders. By the same token, the exclusive use of psychological treatments for spiritual problems is costly and dangerous to the soul.

Ultimately, calling people to respond to God's grace through regeneration has to be our primary focus. After all, "What good will it be for a man if he gains the whole world, yet forfeits his soul?" (Mt. 16:26).

For many, however, evangelism may mean helping them overcome the psychological obstacles to surrendering to this grace. This is where Christian counseling becomes a means of grace.

PART TWO

Counseling Situations

All pastors live squarely on a fault line. The question is not if a crisis will come but when. Even though I can't schedule them, I can, like residents of San Francisco, learn to be prepared.

— *Gary Gulbranson*

CHAPTER FIVE

Crisis Situations

The day I candidated at Glen Ellyn Bible Church, following the Sunday morning service, we were having lunch at the home of the chairman of the board of elders.

Suddenly, in the middle of the meal, the phone rang, and when our host returned, his face was pale.

He quickly gave us the facts: the son of one of the church families, a college-age man who had attended church that morning, had left the service early, gone home, and apparently taken his own life.

We dropped our forks and drove together to the grieving family's home. As others gave comfort to the family, I listened and avoided treading on their grief.

As the afternoon went on, my thoughts turned to the evening service. What I had planned to preach would now be out of place. This was a crisis not only for the immediate family but for the whole church.

After we left their home, I spent the next few hours planning how to lead that service. I chose a different sermon text, 2 Corinthians 1, and outlined a new message. Although prepared at short notice, my ministry that night, by necessity, addressed the pain and grief everyone was feeling.

It was not a typical candidating Sunday. But years later, one of the church elders observed, "When we came to vote on Gary's candidacy the next week, it wasn't a matter of deciding whether or not to call him as our pastor. He already was. We'd been through a crisis together, and he had already proven to be our pastor."

The main point is this: Crises don't come at convenient times. I certainly can't schedule them in my calendar. But they are a critical part of my calling, as much as preaching and administration. Not only do people need care for the devastation already experienced, they need help handling the lingering effects. Crises have the potential to worsen and expand, like the fires and aftershocks that follow a major earthquake.

All pastors live squarely on a fault line. The question is not if a crisis will come but when. Even though I can't schedule them, I can, like residents of San Francisco, learn to be prepared.

Separate Crises from Problems

First we must know what truly is a crisis. If we treat every problem as a crisis, we will be full-time crisis managers. Every pastor has had calls in the middle of the night from people who want immediate attention for relatively minor problems. The key is to be fully available to such people while not overresponding.

If the person calling considers his situation a crisis, then I treat it as one, at least initially. I give such people my full and immediate attention; I respect the feelings and validate the pain they feel; I show I care. And I'm available like this until I can see where things stand.

Empathy at this point is critical. I try to react not based on how I feel about others' problems but on how I would feel if I were in their place. Their mountain may be a molehill, but if they see it as a mountain, I need to help them work through those feelings and get a better perspective.

Communicating such care while assessing the situation may take only five minutes. Then depending on the need, I can set an appointment or make other plans to attend to them. In this way, I can manage the problem without dismissing the person's pain. And if it's an authentic crisis, I can take more immediate action.

Manage Your Own Reaction

I once received a call at 3 A.M. to come and help the family of a man who had just killed himself with a shotgun.

Initially, all they knew was that a shot had been fired and the man was hospitalized. It was my job to drive the wife and her three children to the hospital and then, when I discovered exactly what happened, inform them that the husband/father had taken his own life.

In situations like this, my first challenge is to manage my own reactions.

I typically face two kinds of crises: those I feel confident and qualified to manage because of my experience and training, and those that intimidate me. Each has its own temptations.

When I feel comfortable, I get impatient. I know the nature of the problem before the person stops talking. I know what needs to happen. I know how people tend to respond. And I know how to fix things. I want to start giving advice prematurely.

When I'm intimidated by the situation, I want to do something, anything, because I'm the pastor. I feel like if I don't take control, I'll appear feckless. Under that pressure I usually blunder.

To manage my reactions, I keep two things in mind:

● *I won't be much good to people if their crises become my crises*. In a situation where I can neither touch bottom or keep my head above water, I have to remain calm. If I identify too much with people's fear, panic, and insecurity, I will be unable to minister. I want to be able to feel what they feel, to tell them those feelings are normal, but I want to keep a clear head. How?

My answer is to acquire skills and training. I must have something to offer people. Burnout hits pastors and counselors who repeatedly face situations that outstrip their competence.

When I was in seminary, I also worked as a real estate agent. One day my partner put me in an uneasy situation. A woman who had worked as a waitress with his daughter was dying of cancer. The doctors had told her she had only a few weeks to live. She didn't know Christ.

He said, "You have seminary training. Would you call on her?"

"Yes, I'll gladly see her," I replied. Inside, however, I felt queasy, dubious of my ability to say anything that would help her.

Later I sat in the parking lot of the hospital, marshaling my strength, thinking, *Nothing I have done to this point has prepared me for this*. I prayed and decided the one thing I could do was listen. If nothing else, I could give an attentive ear and pray with her. With that in mind, I walked into the hospital and took the elevator to her room.

It didn't take much small talk to get down to her real need. I said, "I don't know what you're going through, and I really want to hear."

"It started as ovarian cancer," she said. "Then it spread throughout my lower tract. The pain is like the harshest pain a woman goes through in labor, but this one never stops. At first I fought against taking pain medication because I wanted to be clear-minded when I visit with my 13-year-old daughter. But then the pain got to be too much."

By the time we finished talking several hours later, she had prayed to receive Christ. When I walked out of the hospital, I was totally spent. I got in my car and slumped in the seat with my eyes closed. I knew the Lord had helped me minister to this woman, but I also knew I lacked the competence to handle all the issues involved in helping people in crisis. Then and there I decided to learn all the crisis skills I could.

Though I have followed through, I don't always have total control of my emotions, and at times I feel uneasy and at a loss. That's good. It keeps me depending on the Holy Spirit for effectiveness. I never enter a crisis with the idea I'm going to solve it. I use the skills I've learned, yet only as the Holy Spirit applies them to the person in need can they take hold.

● *A crisis is an opportunity.* In a sense I've learned to look forward to crises — not to the harm they cause, but to the good that God brings as a result:

1. People grow. One night a member, Sara, called to tell me her 39-year-old husband was dead. While they were on vacation together, he had suffered a massive heart attack.

She had no one to help her. My wife and I stepped in, and over the next few days became extremely close with her. Up until then, she had been only marginally involved in the church. As she experienced Christ's love through us and the church, she began wanting to share it with others. Now Sara has become heavily involved caring for others in need. Her crisis was a tragedy, but she emerged a stronger person and a more committed believer.

2. Relationships deepen. Most people never forget that the pastor was there in their hour of deepest need. Our family is now as close to Sara as to anyone in the church, although before her crisis I knew her only as the red-headed woman who sat in worship in the third row. After pastors leave a congregation, the people who keep contact with them are often those whom they helped in crisis.

3. A sense of satisfaction fills me. Since crises are part of my calling, and since I have invested considerably in crisis training, I get fireman-like satisfaction from entering the burning houses of people's lives and walking out with them on my shoulder. This isn't the messiah complex at work but a legitimate sense that I am doing

something significant — doing what God called me to do.

I can't immediately see the fruits of other pastoral labor, but when counseling in crisis, I often see tangible results very quickly.

Handling a Crisis

I may not be able to plan for a specific crisis, but I can decide ahead of time what steps I will take once a crisis presents itself. Here is what I try to do:

• *Offer presence.* In the midst of the suicide tragedy on candidating Sunday, one woman from the congregation came to the family home and just sat on the couch with her arm around the shoulder of the grieving mother. For the entire afternoon, I don't think she said ten words. But the mother later told me, "I drew more comfort from her than from anything." Presence is powerful.

Pain and trauma isolate a person, particularly in medical crises. A patient is in alien surroundings, treated by some personnel more like a problem than a person. People in pain want to withdraw, like a turtle into its shell. But isolation intensifies the pain.

So those in crisis first need others to be with them. Meaningful touch, as the woman above showed, helps pull crisis victims out of isolation. Sufferers can dismiss our words. But touch — the language of crisis — has innate authority.

• *Listen attentively.* One of the biggest mistakes a pastor can make is to prescribe answers and solutions in the initial stages of a crisis. At this stage, crisis victims need description, not prescription. So I let them fully describe what has happened, what they're feeling, what they're going through. Few things communicate compassion and concern more than unhurried listening.

This means resisting the temptation to offer even good advice. We all know that clichés usually cause more pain than comfort. When crisis victims hear pat answers, they feel we don't understand the depth of their traumas.

But even truth, given prematurely, can do more harm than good. Although this may be the fiftieth person we've counseled about grief, to the person going through the grief, it feels like a unique experience. So telling a widow "You are not the only one who has experienced this; others in our church have gotten through this, and so will you" only belittles her loss. Later, the person may want to get in touch with others who have gone through the same thing, but in the beginning, the person needs to simply express how this experience is like nothing else.

Sometimes I don't listen well because I prejudge the situation or the person. I did this once with a couple in a marital crisis. They were not a part of the church, so I didn't know anything about them when they came to see me. But the wife, a seething volcano of anger and bitterness, made it difficult to like her from the start. She even made fun of the church, calling our worship a "dog and pony show."

I felt she was a lost cause, and frankly I wanted to get rid of them gracefully. As counseling continued, however, I discovered some of the roots of her anger. She had suffered sexual abuse as a child. The more I learned, the less I wanted to write her off.

Rarely are counseling situations clear from the first session. The longer I counsel, the more I know about human nature, and ironically, the less I feel I can prejudge people. More than ever, I listen for the factors that make this person and problem unique.

• *Clarify the situation.* Medical crises require quick decisions about procedures to be done, organs to be donated, life support systems to be used.

A death forces kin into dozens of decisions about funeral arrangements, the distribution of possessions, living arrangements, financial planning, and legal matters.

Unemployment requires a person to reassess retirement, education, self-identity, and where to live.

Crisis victims have to make many major, life-changing decisions, and usually in a compressed period of time. One such decision alone is stressful. Add many together, and it's bewildering. Tack on emotional shock, and it's crushing.

Not surprisingly, decision-making can cause people in crisis to freeze. They desperately need someone who can objectively identify the issues, sort the priorities, and clarify values.

When a person in church loses a loved one, I drop everything and go to the family. I also accompany the family at the funeral home and inform them, "I want to help you understand what the funeral director is doing." We go into the casket room, and I help them clarify what it means to buy a casket, that their feelings for their loved one don't have to be expressed in a lavish casket. I help them assemble documents.

I've learned a key principle about how assertive I can be in helping a family deal with doctors, funeral directors, and lawyers: If these professionals are not making sense to me, they are almost certainly not making sense to the crisis victim, who is normally too intimidated to ask many questions. So I ask on his or her behalf. And because I've gone through these things before, I can help interpret the technical language and procedures and decisions.

These aren't the only things I clarify. People need help interpreting their feelings. Is anger the fountainhead of this man's marriage problems, or is anger masking guilt over some failing? Is the broken woman at a funeral simply grieving her loss or resenting her increased responsibilities? The job of clarification and interpretation is one of our most important.

• *Do damage control.* Crises can easily get out of control. Most people can deal with only one crisis at a time, but every crisis has the ability to spawn other emotional, financial, occupational, family, and identity crises. Victims can quickly lose hope. When a person is vulnerable, when everything is already shaky, crises' "offspring" can do incredible damage.

Take marital arguments. One couple came to me right after the wife learned of her husband's adulterous relationship. He had been involved for three years with his secretary. I knew I wasn't going to save their marriage in one session, but I did need to contain the forest fire.

First, I wanted to keep them from tearing each other apart. In addition, they had three kids. I knew she probably wanted to march home and say, "Look what your father has done." She probably wanted to call up the other woman, whom she knew well, and tell her off. She could have kindled an inferno. She could have moved out of the house and cut herself off from everyone. Each of these could have created additional crises, and that was the last thing they needed right then.

So in that first visit, we addressed the bare minimum. I needed to hear their story, trace how the adultery developed, and let her initial anger and his defensiveness blaze in a place where they couldn't incinerate each other. She needed to hear me say, "It's right for you to be angry at him." He needed to hear, "What you've done has not irreparably harmed your marriage or your life. There's still hope for you." And we tried to contain the flames to the smallest possible area.

Two years later, they are holding their own. They're still clearing away some of the charred timber, but they're making it.

• *Show the next step.* A woman called me and, sobbing, said, "I have to see you today." I agreed to see her immediately. When she came in, I learned she was suffering intolerable guilt over two abortions received before committing her life to Christ. In a single day, due to a conversation she'd had with a friend who didn't know her situation, it became a crippling issue.

In that first meeting, I assured her of Christ's forgiveness and began to walk her through the grieving process. As we finished that session, I assured her, "Let's talk again next week." Her emotions were so tender, I knew she would require consistent support to keep her from tumbling back into debilitating guilt.

People in crisis tremble before a dark future; they need light shed on the next step. They need to look forward to care and attention in the immediate future. So I always conclude my initial care with "I'll call you tonight," or "We'll meet at my office on Tuesday at three o'clock." I specify what I'm going to do next, and I don't put that too far in the future. How far depends on how they have responded to my initial attention.

I don't overwhelm them with a detailed plan for solving the crisis. I tell them, "We're going to take this one step at a time." Most can't see much beyond the next step anyway.

Recognize the Uniqueness of Various Crises

As much as all crises require a similar approach, not all crises are alike. Each type of crisis requires unique skills, attention, and focus:

- *Death.* In addition to listening and empathy, I find people are helped by knowing the stages of grief. That way their mercurial emotions aren't so baffling to them.

- *Domestic violence.* Over the years, many abused wives have called me saying they've been beaten, and they're afraid it could happen again. We don't waste time scheduling an appointment for this afternoon at three. Instead, I tell her to call the police and get to a shelter, where I will make contact with her.

I give immediate and specific direction with domestic violence because the victim has a confused, skewed understanding of her situation. Women often feel responsible. In addition, after being hit, they assume, *Well, this was an isolated thing. It won't happen again. Things will get better.* But things usually get worse.

- *Child abuse.* The law requires I report any abuse I have witnessed or heard about. But when it comes to relaying second-hand information, I only report what I have witnessed or heard: "A woman reported to me today that her child is regularly beaten by the woman's husband" not "I know a child who is being beaten by his father." It's the legal system's job to figure out exactly what's going on. It's my legal responsibility to report what I've heard.

- *Marriage conflict.* Anger is often the biggest roadblock to progress. After letting a husband and wife vent anger at one another, I try to get them to take a step back to see a long-term solution to their crisis. Only then can we can begin working constructively.

- *Loss of job.* For the unemployed, a large part of the crisis is self-identity. A man, especially, assumes all the family's financial responsibility is his, and he's dropped the ball. Since society says, "A man is what a man does," he feels like a loser. He may even be hearing that from his wife or kids.

I have two immediate objectives in these cases. First, I help the person feel worth outside of his or her ability to provide financially.

Second, I find the immediate financial pressure point — a mortgage payment, a tax penalty — and help the person figure out how to deal with it.

- *Threatened suicide.* Most people who threaten suicide feel they've lost control of everything — except death. So the last thing I do is try to wrest control from them by saying, "Don't do it. It's wrong. Think of all the people you would hurt." That just reinforces their despair.

I let them take control, even in the conversation. "Tell me what's going on in your life." I affirm the one positive action they've just taken: calling me — "It was great of you to reach out to someone. It's important for you to do that." I let them feel they've taken some control of their lives already, that calling was a good thing.

Since the early days of my ministry, I have intentionally sought opportunities to help people in crisis. I have volunteered as chaplain of hospitals and with the police and fire departments. I have gone out of my way to build a network of relationships outside of the church, in organizations such as Rotary Club, so that people in the community with a crisis but without a pastor can call me. I emphasize to the congregation that despite the size of our church, I am available in a crisis.

Why bring more problems upon myself? Crises are life-defining, path-setting moments for people. If someone stands at their side, representing Christ and offering compassionate help, they often will draw closer to God. And that, finally, is what my ministry is about.

I find it is not only possible but imperative, especially in short-term counseling, that we start solving problems in the very first session.

— Jim Smith

CHAPTER SIX

Short-term Care

Short-term counseling may be short, but it's not necessarily simple.

Jenny's daughter was getting married, and Jenny wasn't happy. Of course, Jenny recognized that her daughter Lynn, who was in her late twenties, was old enough to make her own decisions. Jenny also knew that Lynn was marrying a Christian young man with a good career. But Jenny still wasn't happy.

For one thing, Lynn had announced that the wedding would take place in just two months. That gave Jenny hardly any time to plan. She had always dreamed of Lynn's wedding as the event that would make everyone forget Prince Charles and Lady Di — a thousand guests, a lavish reception at the finest country club in Dallas. But with the event only two months away, there was no time to plan the wedding of Jenny's dreams. The dream was scaled down to a backyard wedding with 300 guests.

Moreover, Lynn's fiancé was not exactly everything Jenny had hoped for in a son-in-law. Before becoming a Christian, he had been involved with drugs and a wild lifestyle with the wrong kind of people. Though he had straightened out in recent years, he was a young man with an unsavory past, whereas Jenny's daughter, Lynn, had been raised in a sheltered, white-bread, suburban environment.

When Jenny came, she was grieving her dream. "If Lynn would only wait a few more months," she told me, "it could be such a beautiful wedding. But she says she doesn't want a big wedding. She just wants to be married to Scott. Why are young people always in such a hurry? They have so many years to spend together, but they have to get married in a rush."

"Parenting has its limitations," I said. "It's hard enough to influence the will of a toddler. But Lynn's a full-blown adult, with the right to live her life as she pleases — and even to make a mess of her life, if that's what she wants. You can talk to her and share your perspective, but she's calling the shots now."

I talked with her about the parable of the Prodigal Son, and about how Jesus packaged that parable with the stories of the lost coin and the lost sheep. She took some encouragement from these parables. "I know I need to let go, that I can't run her life," she said. "And I'm grateful for the fact that my relationship with Lynn is strong — even though we can both be hard-headed at times."

We talked together for the better part of an hour. I listened carefully not only to Jenny's expressed feelings, but also for the hidden emotions she might not even be aware of. In the end, we both agreed that she would have to do her grief work while publicly being as happy for Lynn as she could. She left my office determined to make the best of what was in her mind a very imperfect situation.

A lot was involved in that short encounter. It was not a matter of simply consoling a concerned mother. A number of skills and personal experiences helped shape how I handled that.

In fact, short-term counseling is one of the most effective ways I help people, provided I keep a few things in mind.

Short-term Versus Long-term Counseling

I need to keep in mind the difference between the purposes of short- and long-term counseling.

The goal of long-term psychotherapy is to bring about basic changes in the habits of the counselee. And this process of breaking down old patterns and installing new ones takes a great deal of time.

Short-term counseling can be a powerful and effective tool for helping people in immediate emotional and spiritual trouble. It usually involves addressing some sort of immediate crisis or event in the counselee's life, helping people through the aftermath of a significant loss or through an important transition — job loss, grief, torn friendships, loneliness, parenting problems, marital disputes. And short-term counseling by definition is brief: four to eight weeks.

Premarital counseling is perhaps the most common situation in which pastors do short-term counseling. Premarital counseling is usually not focused on a pathology. Rather, the goal is to map out the road ahead for two people embarking on the journey of life's second greatest commitment.

I see myself as a river guide to people who are about to take a white-water rafting trip (a pretty close approximation to marriage at times). Telling a couple, "There are some rapids two miles downstream, but the rough water won't last long, so don't panic," helps steady them through the turbulent waters.

I also want to establish a relationship so that the couple will be willing to turn to me when, down the stream, things become too bumpy for them to handle themselves. And in four or five visits, such limited but important goals can be met.

Assessing the Situation

The first task, then, is to determine whether the person in my office needs short-term or long-term counseling. So, in the first counseling session, as I listen to the counselee, I ask myself a number of questions. If I answer no to most if not all of these questions, then I'm probably safe in approaching it as a short-term counseling situation.

• Is there an on-going family or personal conflict going on in this person's life? Is there a repeated pattern in this issue?

• Is addiction evident in this problem?

• Is there evidence of obsessive/compulsive behavior with this problem?

• Is there a long-term pattern of abnormal behavior?

• Is this an issue that requires a specialist?

Suppose a man comes in for counseling and says, "Pastor, I've had an affair. I feel shame and guilt. I feel I've betrayed not only my wife but my kids, my church, and my Lord as well. What can I do?" I mustn't assume anything about this man and his affair. I have to ask questions like: Was this affair a "one night stand"? Is it an on-going relationship? Is it part of a long-term habit in which he moves from affair to affair with a succession of women?

The man who falls into sexual temptation for the first and only time during his twenty years of marriage is an entirely different case from the man who has been using sexual promiscuity as a way of building his ego or proving his masculinity or comforting himself.

Both men need to find God's forgiveness, but the second man needs to understand what is driving him to his bed-hopping lifestyle. He has a problem with compulsive behavior, and he needs some long-term psychotherapeutic counseling to understand why he does what he does.

The first man needs simply to understand what led to his one fall and what steps he can take to prevent that happening again.

Another key question in the first session is *Are there multigenerational issues involved?* In the field of addiction, for example, some studies indicate that people can be tilted toward addictive behavior by both genetic and environmental factors.

In terms of this man's infidelity, I might find that his problems are part of a family pattern: his father was a womanizer; his sister has been promiscuous all her adult life; his brother has been married six times. It quickly becomes apparent he was raised in a family that did not produce emotionally healthy people.

This is a very different case from the person who says, "I came from such a good family, and I'm ashamed of the way I've violated my upbringing."

Sometimes, then, the answers to these questions point to hidden issues, lurking under the surface of the counselee's awareness, like the hidden bulk of an iceberg. But sometimes it's a simple case of "what you see is what you get." Some problems are just a matter of bad timing, bad judgment, or poor choices. These problems can often be corrected with four or five hours of counseling.

The Pastor's Biggest Temptation

During that first session, the pastor faces a grave temptation: to ease people's pain.

Eloise comes in for grief counseling. Roger, her husband of over thirty years, died two weeks ago. I help her with her grief. I pray with her. I share Scripture with her and reassure her of the reality of heaven and the resurrection. I relieve her pain. I send her on her way.

And I do her a tragic disservice.

In Eloise's case, there was more than grief to deal with. She was enmeshed with her husband Roger in an unhealthy way. She had submerged her own identity within his. She had never had a life of her own. Now she's beginning to transfer her dependence to her son. There are major issues of codependency involved. Yet, in my eagerness to salve Eloise's pain, I missed all these other issues. There is a malignancy growing in Eloise's life, and I have handed her a Band-Aid.

We pastors are generally a tenderhearted lot. Sometimes

we're so anxious to get people out of their pain we make the biggest mistake of all — missing a long-term symptom while doing short-term counseling. In fact, if there is one mistake I regret more than any other in my pastoral career, it is the mistake of being too eager to move people out of their pain when it would have been better to leave them there just a little longer.

I've learned never to assume anything, never to jump to the conclusion that a situation only needs some prayer and some biblical reassurance. People often hide the core issues of their problems even from themselves. By letting people off the hook too quickly, we become unwitting accomplices in their denial, their compulsions, and their sins.

Another example: a single woman comes in hurting because she is sleeping around. She is embarrassed and ashamed and condemning herself. It is tempting to jump in and try to relieve her shame, offer her God's forgiveness, and get her to stop being so hard on herself, but the question I should really be asking her is, "Why are you beating up on yourself? Why do you keep going back to this behavior you despise so much?" It would be a major mistake to rush in and give her an anesthetic before I find out where she hurts and why.

Expectations and Assignments

Assessing the problem is the key task in the first session — but it is not the only task. Once I've determined that counseling will be short-term, I immediately get to work.

First, I need to determine what the counselee expects to happen in our sessions.

In marital counseling, for example, I ask both the husband and the wife each to summarize the problem as they see it. Then I ask how each would like their marriage to be different. That tells me what they expect (or at least hope) to achieve in counseling. Sometimes I'll write those expectations on the blackboard so that we can fix the goal firmly in our minds.

Then I set a contract with the couple for a counseling term of between four to eight sessions. At the end of that term, we can determine together whether we want to renew the contract for another four to eight weeks.

Having a definite time frame tends to focus everyone's mind on the task at hand. It also eases the counselee's anxiety: Many people are apprehensive about counseling because they fear it may go on forever, draining their time and resources without ever achieving closure. Short-term counseling should take place within limits that are agreed upon at the outset.

In short-term counseling, my goal is to help counselees understand (1) why they do what they do, (2) what they would like to do differently, and (3) how to do things differently. Assignments move us more quickly to that last goal; so by the end of the first session, I usually assign projects during the week.

Giving the counselee an assignment is especially important in short-term counseling, because we have only a limited number of 50-minute sessions to get the problem out in the open and resolve or manage it. Assignments help both the counselor and counselee "cut to the chase" and quickly expose the issue. I use three types:

• *Readings.* If the counselee needs to understand better his childhood, for instance, I may assign a book that describes various parenting styles and the kinds of problems those styles often engender in adult life. The counselee can read that book at home and get insight into whether he was over-indulged, over-corrected, neglected, driven toward over-perfectionism, and the like. The next time we get together, the counselee has already progressed a few miles down the road toward understanding his problem.

• *Journaling.* A journal forces a person to consciously reflect on her choices and feelings. Sometimes I ask a counselee to record her self-talk during the day: Am I down on myself — or my own best encourager? Am I upbeat about the future — or a defeatist? A journal gives us a record of moods and attitudes, almost like an emotional electrocardiogram.

Some people, particularly those who are in an addictive cycle, journal almost hourly. (Although most compulsions require long-term counseling, some can be dealt with effectively in four or five weeks.) They carry a pad or a book with them and record their thoughts, feelings, temptations and compulsions, and the things that worked (or didn't work) in dealing with those temptations and compulsions. It's a way of forcing themselves to live consciously, reflectively, and volitionally instead of merely drifting through life on the autopilot of their destructive habits.

● *Homework.* These are tasks I ask people to undertake to help them grapple with their problems.

In counseling couples filled with anger and resentment against one another, for instance, I might try to find small ways to reverse that hostility and immediately get things moving in the right direction.

For example, I'll tell the husband that he has to do something very special for his wife at least once a day until our next session. He has to write it down on a list that he will bring to the next counseling session. But he's not allowed to announce to his partner, "Here's your goody for the day." The wife has to do the same.

This assignment does several things. It gets each partner focused on the needs of the other. It begins a pattern of kindness toward each other; often, kind feelings will follow kind acts, and healing will begin to take place. It also gives the couple hope. They begin to think, *Maybe we're not doomed to divorce after all. Maybe there's just a chance we can work this thing out.*

Without such an assignment, the couple would come in and dump their hostility on my office floor, then leave feeling as angry and bitter as when they came. When couples are in conflict, it's vitally important to get the healing started as soon as possible.

● *Writing.* This is a little different than journaling in that I pose a number of questions and ask the counselee to come to the next session prepared to discuss the answers to these questions. For example:

— What was the warmest room in the house, emotionally speaking, when you were growing up?

— Think of your mother. What are some key words that come to mind when you think of your mother?

— Think of your father. What are some key words that come to mind when you think of your father?

— How did your parents feel about money?

— How did your parents feel about sex?

— Who was the chief disciplinarian in your home? How did that person feel about the disciplinary role?

These questions get at much of the same information I would otherwise seek in the counseling hour, but I'm able to progress with the counselee much more quickly by giving these questions as a writing assignment.

While some therapists believe that the first counseling session should be spent just gathering information, I find it is not only possible but imperative, especially in short-term counseling, that we start exploring solutions in the first session. I want to build hope in the very first hour, and assignments are one of the tools for building hope. Assignments give counselees a sense that they're already moving forward, the process is in motion, and insights are beginning to surface.

Intentions

In the first session, I try to find out what help the counselee expects to receive from me. In the second, I try to discover what counselees intend to bring to the process themselves. The second session has to answer this question: How serious is the counselee?

I assess the counselee's seriousness by asking how he or she did with the assignment I gave in the first session.

If the counselee has read or journaled or done homework as I assigned and returns to the second session brimming with insights and understanding, then I have a pretty good idea that the counselee's intentions are sincere. The counselee is prepared to work, and so we continue.

But sometimes counselees haven't done the assignment — "I just didn't have time," they'll say. Then it's time for me to explore a little and respond according to what I discover. The main reasons for not completing assignments are these:

• *Sloth.* After a little discussion, I sometimes sense the counselee is just lazy. So I'll respond, "Are you really serious about what we're doing here? Is this a priority in your life or are we just kidding each other? Are you being honest with me and with yourself about your commitment to wholeness?" Often that awakes them, and they begin taking their problems more seriously.

• *Looking for magic solutions.* Some people come and nearly expect me to wave a magic wand over them and make their problems go away. Such people need to have a bucket of cold reality splashed in their faces. I sometimes ask, "Do you realize that marriage takes work? Or do you expect me to do all the work for you?"

If a couple says to me, "We just want to feel good, to have those passionate feelings we had when we were first married," I'll reply, "Well, gee, last week I accidentally sat on my magic wand and broke it."

In fact, a counselor friend of mine has an actual wand — a stick with glitter and stars on it — that he pulls out and waves over people when they make such statements, just to show them how ludicrous their expectations are.

• *Avoidance of pain.* Sometimes people seek an anesthetic for the symptoms not a cure for the disease.

Some people, for instance, are desperately lonely. They come for counseling because they view the pastor as a genial father or caring friend. They tend to avoid the homework assignments because those assignments make them face the pain of their loneliness.

Often, such people are difficult to keep in therapy. The moment you are able to soothe their pain to a point where they can stand it, they disappear. They were never really there to make changes in their habits and their attitudes. They just came in to get their level of pain down to a tolerable threshold. If you confront their pain too boldly, they'll feel threatened and drop out.

Such people, then, need to be dealt with gently but still directly: "I'm concerned that you didn't do your assignment. I imagine it was painful to deal with, but unless you're willing to do the assignments, it's not going to do much good to continue to see me."

• *Outright resistance.* Some counselees display anger or irritation with the assignment: "This assignment was stupid! I came here to feel better, not to get loaded down with a lot of ridiculous homework. I'm not in the seventh grade, for crying out loud!"

In such cases, I try to find out who else they've been resisting and who I represent to them — mother, father, spouse?

In any event, strong resistance to homework assignments tells me that the counselee's defense mechanisms have kicked in — and that's a clue that deep, long-term emotional forces are at work in the counselee's issues, and that usually means referral.

These people too must be handled gently: "You know, I asked you to do some very simple things for your own insight and benefit, and you appear to be very resistant to doing them. I sense your resistance is actually part of the problem. I sense that your issues are going to require some long-term help, so I would like to refer you to someone who is very good at helping people with these kinds of issues."

I'm available to help people in any way I can — to identify and clarify their issues. But I don't heal anybody. God and the counselee must do the work of healing. If counselees are willing to work, change will take place. If not, I can't do the work for them. People have to solve their own problems.

Closure

Howard is a successful attorney. Several years ago, he sat in my office with his wife June, weeping and moaning and calling himself "a failure." His salary could have fed, clothed, and housed five median-income families in my church, yet he and his wife were drowning in debt and headed for bankruptcy court. They had no idea where their money went, so in one of our early sessions, I gave them the assignment of making out a budget.

The next week they came to my office, and I asked to see the budget. They hemmed and hawed and made this and that excuse. So I grabbed a pad of paper and said, "Look, this is not brain surgery. It's just a family budget. I'm getting the sense that the two of you just don't want to deal with reality. So we're going to draw up a budget right now. Howard, how much do you make?"

"A hundred-fifty K."

"Good. Now that puts you in the 28 percent bracket, so let's just take off $42,000 for Uncle Sam. That leaves $108,000."

"Well, I have to pay my own Social Security," he said, and I figured that in. "And there's my pension," he added, and I subtracted a little more. He spoke and I wrote until we had whittled his income down to about $94,000 of disposable income. We divided that by 12, which came out to about $7,800 for Howard and June to spend each month. Then we added up all their fixed costs for each month, and those figures totaled $8,500. We discovered that they were hemorrhaging at a rate of $700 a month.

"Now you can see," I said, "why you are going in the hole to the tune of $700 dollars a month — a total of over $8,000 a year."

"But I make $150,000 dollars a year!" Howard protested.

"Howard," I said, "you don't make $150,000. You make less than $8,000 a month."

Then I saw a light come on in Howard's eyes — and June's. "I think I finally understand," said June. "I've been thinking Howard makes $150,000, and that anyone making that kind of money is entitled to a certain kind of lifestyle. I never looked at it in terms of finite numbers before."

As we continued talking, it became clear that a large part of the problem was that June had been treating credit cards as a source of unlimited wealth. She had been raised in an extremely affluent environment, and she had always used her father's credit cards as a kind of magical money tree that paid all the bills. She had never in her life had to think in terms of a limited amount of income. Sitting in my office with the facts staring her in the face, she frowned and said, "I really have to deal with this."

I said, "Yes, you do. We have worked out a budget of so-called "fixed" expenses that exceeds your spendable income. But I have a feeling a lot of these fixed expenses are really optional. The two of you can live on the money Howard makes. Ninety-five percent of the people in this country live on considerably less. But you are going to have to make those choices. You are going to have to eliminate many of those expenses so that you can get to a point where you are living on a thousand or two less than you make each month and start paying off your debts."

I could see that my words were painful to them, and they were exhibiting some resistance. I added, "If you choose to live in reality, it will take you only about five years to get out of the fix you are in. But if you choose not to live in reality, if you clutch the illusion that you are making $150,000 a year, you will be filing Chapter Seven within twelve months. It's your call. I'm not going to come to your house every month and lecture you and help you pay your bills. You have the ability to put your financial house in order. Only you can decide to do that."

At that point, our hour was over. I had done all I could. We had uncovered the facts and recorded those facts on paper. They had a copy of the budget, and I kept a copy for my records, so we wouldn't have to go over it again in the future. They knew what they had to do.

We had reached a point of closure.

Closure doesn't mean happily ever after. It doesn't mean the problems are all wrapped up and tied with a bow. Closure means that insights have surfaced, choices have been clarified, and the counselee can now see the road to wholeness. Whether the counselee chooses to walk that road or not is up to the counselee, not the pastor.

When I get to the end of a course of counseling, I ask the counselee:

● What has been helpful to you?

● Where have we gotten?

● How have your hopes and expectations been met? And how have we failed to meet them?

● What changes have you made in your life as a result of these counseling visits?

The final session is a time to summarize the past and look to the future. It is also a time when I let the counselee know that the door is open if he or she ever needs a return session. "This issue may resurface in the future," I say. "If you want to come back and talk with me, you are welcome to do so."

It is also a time to point the counselee to additional resources that will keep the healing process going — books, tape series, an adult Christian education class on Sunday mornings, or support groups and organizations such as Alanon or Alateen. I also pray with the counselee — a prayer that affirms the counselee's desire for continued healing and that asks for God's grace for the road ahead.

The rewards and satisfactions of short-term counseling don't become apparent in the short term. Rather, these rewards and satisfactions are like diamonds embedded in layers of time, in the bedrock of relationships.

Wholeness is not a destination. It's a journey. In this life we never arrive; we're always in process. Everyone in my congregation is in process. I am in process. Life is a process. We face our struggles one at a time, day by day, and only at the end of a year or ten years or twenty can we see the progress we've made.

So I can't always see results at the end of a four-week or eight-week course of counseling. But when over the years, I see individuals, couples, and families growing strong, their relationships knitting together, their kids maturing free of addiction and shame — that's rewarding.

Long-term counseling gives me the unparalleled opportunity to witness firsthand the subtle yet powerful healing that God brings.

— Archibald Hart

Long-term Care

Long-term counseling can be long indeed. Take the case of an elderly woman who had been seeing me for eight and a half years.

About twenty years earlier, she had been given the conservatorship of her wealthy, elderly parents. However, about a year into the conservatorship, her parents sued her, alleging that she was defrauding their estate. Naturally, she denied the accusation, and it didn't go anywhere in the courts.

But shortly after, the daughter developed chronic pain. She felt pain in nearly every part of her body. She would have surgery for one problem only to discover the pain had moved elsewhere. After ten years of testing, research, and operations in a major research hospital, it was determined the problem was psychogenic. She was referred to me.

So I employed the usual procedures: we tried biofeedback and relaxation training; we explored her early childhood. But nothing new was revealed, and the pain continued. After a few years of seemingly no progress, I suggested we break off therapy. But she insisted we continue. I tried again each year to break it off, but each year she insisted we continue.

Then one day — about eight and a half years into counseling — she froze as a glimmer of truth shone momentarily into her consciousness. She realized that she had, in fact, stolen from her parent's estate.

It was a classic case of repression: the thought that she could rob from her own parents was so unacceptable that she totally repressed the thought, and that had gotten converted into serious pain.

Now I was confronted with a very emotionally disturbed person. She had learned something about herself, but she didn't know what to do with it. There was no going to her parents; they were dead by then. She wondered, *What do I do now? Go to the police? I'd rather hang myself. I cannot live with this embarrassment, this shame.*

It was a delicate stage in our counseling. Her shame could have acted as a trigger for a serious breakdown, or more tragically, suicide.

In fact, we were able to move quickly from shame, to guilt, to forgiveness, so that within a year and a half, the woman told me she was ready to stop counseling. Today she lives in a retirement community with her husband, free from her physical and psychological pain.

This is long-term counseling at its longest and most satisfying. It's an extreme case that a pastor is not likely to get into. But it illustrates well many of the dynamics that pastors face in long-term counseling.

The Limits of the Long

First we must define what long-term counseling is for a typical pastor. That's best done by comparing it to short-term counseling.

Short-term counseling deals with crisis intervention (death in the family, divorce, loss of a job) or supporting and guiding people through significant transitions (marriage, retirement). The problem is circumscribed (e.g., helping a parent deal with a rebellious teenager, or showing an employee how to get along better with his boss) — it doesn't require a major adjustment in personality to resolve.

Long-term counseling goes a layer deeper into a person's psyche. It tries to help people with serious psychological problems (e.g., depression or schizophrenia) to function normally. It usually involves reconstructing some part of a person's personality.

As a general rule, the more severe the problem, the longer counseling is needed. That usually means the earlier a problem is created in a person's life, the longer that counseling is needed. Serious child abuse cases, for example, clearly need long-term counseling.

Also, if a problem has biological roots, then long-term counseling is likely in order. A pastor I was counseling had a serious sexual disorder, and I concluded that ultimately his problem could be traced back to an over-energized sexual drive. This man's sexual genes were just out of control.

In addition, some depressions, like Premenstrual Syndrome, are biologically based, resulting from hormonal changes not psychological issues.

To put it another way, long-term counseling focuses more on the unconscious than the conscious. The unconscious is all the stuff we're unaware of, both psychological motives and biological forces that control us without us knowing it. Short-term counseling works with the apparent and redirects and channels it. Long-term counseling focuses more on discovering what's hidden.

That's the qualitative difference. In terms of time, and in terms of a pastor's work, short-term counseling deals with problems that can be handled in two to six weeks; long-term counseling may require up to a year or two.

Long-term counseling affords sufficient time for a pastor to build trust with a counselee, for the counselee to be willing to open the deeper dimensions of his or her life to the pastor, so that together they can explore the unconscious roots of the person's problems.

When to Take a Long-Term Case

Most pastors are not trained in unveiling the unconscious motives and drives of counselees. And even when trained, they have many demands placed upon them that preclude much, if any, long-term counseling. Still, there are occasions when it is wise for a pastor to counsel long-term.

● *No adequate referral is available.* When a person with serious problems comes along, most pastors will want to refer the person to a competent professional. But some pastors can't do so because they live in a community in which pastors, in fact, are the most competent professional counselors.

Other pastors can't find a theologically sympathetic counselor to whom to refer people. So rather than risk doing more harm than good to the person's faith, the pastor may want to undertake the counseling responsibilities.

● *The client can't afford professional care.* Pastoral counseling is often the only counseling offered gratis to the community. Although some churches charge for counseling on a sliding scale, often they are the only ones willing to slide off the scale completely to help.

● *The pastor is in a rut in short-term counseling.* Every once in a while it's important to see the deeper dynamics that work in people's lives. That will shape how the pastor counsels the short-term client, even if he or she decides to keep the counseling short term; it will also help the pastor better spot long-term problems that need long-term counseling.

No matter the reason though, the pastor who decides to take a client long term will want to get as much training as possible in working with the subconscious. He or she should also have available, in the community or long distance, a professional with whom regular consultation can be made.

Problems to Avoid

No matter the circumstances of the pastor and potential counselee, there are some problems pastors should not counsel.

● *Severe personality disorders.* These require such special understanding and unique treatment that pastors are better off not taking people with these problems. Among the most problematic are the paranoid, histrionic, and borderline personalities (see *The Diagnostic and Statistical Manual of Mental Disorders*, Third edition, revised. Published by the American Psychiatric Association, 1987.

For example, borderline personalities can be vindictive, erratic, and seductive. They also are great manipulators.

One borderline personality I was working with started to manipulate me in two ways. First, when things weren't getting better immediately, she threatened lawsuits. Second, she would repeatedly threaten to commit suicide.

She knew, for instance, that Sunday night at 9:30 I relished watching Masterpiece Theater, my favorite program of the week at the time. Well, one Sunday night, right in the middle of the show, I received a telephone call from my answering service: "A patient in serious trouble needs to talk to you immediately."

It turned out to be this woman. So I phoned her and asked, "What's the problem?"

"I'm going to take my life," she said. "I'm sitting here right now with a razor blade in my hand; I'm going to cut my wrists, right at this moment, while I'm talking to you."

Since I knew this woman and her pathology, and since this was a recurring pattern, I replied directly: "You're not to interrupt me during Masterpiece Theater. You call my office tomorrow and set up an appointment."

You've got to be able to sleep after you've done that. You've got to be absolutely sure of your diagnosis. And that comes from training and experience with this type of pathology. Other people will call up 9:30 Sunday night and say, "I have a razor blade in my hand; I'm going to cut my wrists," and I'll say, "Please don't. I'll see you in ten minutes."

Unless the pastor has such training and experience, such people will likely manipulate the pastor into states of anxiety and guilt that will undermine his or her ability to do other ministry.

• *Immoral Compulsions.* Problems in which psychological compulsion is mixed with moral wrong may need, at first, to be addressed apart from the moral weight of the church. It may be better then, that pastors, who represent the church, refer such cases.

For example, sexuality issues — gender identity, homosexuality, transsexualism, addiction to pornography — tend to produce deep guilt in people. In some cases, they need to deal with the guilt issues directly, and a pastor may be the best person to do that.

In other cases, the guilt issue masks the underlying pathology, and the pastor's role as a representative of the church and its moral standards will find that it gets in the way of effective therapy. In these cases, such people ought to be referred to a non-pastoral counselor.

I've counseled with many men who are troubled by a compulsive use of pornography. They have become addicted to it. In dealing with such men, I've had to separate the moral aspects of their behavior (use of pornography) from their psychological disturbance (compulsivity), in order to bring them to the place of healing.

I have to set aside any judgmental attitude in order to gain their trust and build a therapeutic relationship. This means that I do not always point out the immoral nature of their behavior. This would only create further guilt and interfere with our relationship. I focus on the neurotic, underlying disturbance in their personality.

A pastor cannot always counsel a person this way. It is difficult to willingly set aside Christian standards. In fact, it is necessary for pastors at times to condemn certain behavior simply to be consistent.

Actually then, the pastor who provides a moral conscience collaborates with and counterbalances the counselor, who must provide a non-judgmental atmosphere so that a client will practice self-exploration. Both pastor and counselor are needed for the healing process, but in some cases it is nearly impossible for the same person to serve both functions.

Particularly Appropriate Cases

If pastors are not the appropriate people to take on some long-term cases, they are especially appropriate to take on others.

● *People with distortions about God.* I counseled one woman who told me, "I can't close my eyes in prayer and visualize God without my father's face sneering down at me, wagging his finger at me. I can't pray, 'Our Father . . .' without breaking out in a sweat."

Unfortunately this woman is not alone. Many people, because of verbal or sexual abuse by their fathers, have a distorted image of God. Such people need long-term counseling to deal with their past and their God. And a pastor is in a better situation than a counselor to help people reshape their image of God.

● *Sufferers from guilt.* Many guilt-related problems are also appropriate for a pastor to work with.

I worked with one mother whose teenage daughter shot and killed her father and then herself. The mother was left carrying the guilt. "What did I do wrong?" she plaintively asked me.

Obviously, I take on such cases, but I think it's especially appropriate for a pastor to counsel such people. Ultimately, guilt — healthy guilt, not neurotic guilt — is a theological issue, a topic the pastor is better trained to address. A pastor also has unique liturgical resources — services of confession and public worship — that can help people realize God's forgiveness.

The Importance of an Agenda

In short-term counseling, the crisis often determines the agenda. Pastors make a big mistake, however, if they follow that same pattern in long-term counseling.

Without a plan, sessions can get easily sidetracked and never get back to the starting point. This is especially true if the client is not paying for the sessions. A lot of time can be wasted, both for the pastor and the counselee.

In fact, no matter where on the counseling-theory continuum a counselor falls, it's important to have an agenda for each session and for the overall process. This is even true of those who practice Rogerian therapy, a seemingly non-directive counseling in which the counselor "just" listens. On the surface, this method seems to put total responsibility on the client for determining the agenda. In practice, however, the counselor still sets the agenda for each session, although in close cooperation with the client.

In any case, an agenda is vital. A surgeon has to have a plan before an operation or a series of operations: "I'm going to open his chest and get to his heart; then I'll open his leg and find two good veins, remove them, then . . ." So a therapist has to have a plan, a strategy.

For example, a man in his mid-fifties comes to see me. He says, "I'm in my third marriage, and it's falling apart. I just don't seem to be able to make a go of marriage. The moment I get involved, the moment I marry, somehow the relationship turns sour; I get autocratic, domineering. I get jealous, and the woman just ups and leaves. I desperately want to have a good marriage. I want to be close to someone. Can you help me?"

After our first session, I must begin setting an agenda, at least for the next session. First though, I must determine the extent of the problem; I may even use a sheet or two of paper to write out my analysis: "It's a relationship problem, especially with women. He doesn't treat women with respect. The behavior is technically within normal limits: he's never beaten the woman; he's never been in trouble with the police. His wife just doesn't like his attitude. She doesn't like his manner, the lack of respect. And so, these women up and leave." And so forth.

Then I determine what I think the overall goal of the counseling should be: "Ultimately I want this man to be able to have a happy and lasting marriage. The immediate goal then, is to help this man better relate to women."

With that plan in mind, I'll determine what we should do for the next session: "First, we have to explore his history, especially his first and second marriages."

At the end of that first session, I may suspect that we need to explore his relationship to his mother, how as a child he related to his mother, whether his mother was domineering, and so on.

At the end of that session, I may discover that he had a reasonably normal relationship with his mother, so then I'll want to move forward in his life. The agenda for each of the next twenty sessions, then, cannot be spelled out session by session. But each session will be planned within the context of the larger plan. And at the end of each therapy session, I put in my notes a reminder of what should be the focus of the next week.

The plan should be dynamic, of course. I usually use the first part of the session as an update, to see what's happened to the counselee in the past week. Sometimes I find there's been a crisis (a death, a serious argument, an accident), and that will have to be attended to. And if I have the larger plan, I needn't worry that such events will sidetrack us. We know where we're headed, and we know we've made a temporary stop to deal with some unrelated issues. Soon enough we'll be back on the road.

In addition, I like to share as much of the overall plan as possible with clients. I like them to know where we are in the process. This helps them stay hopeful, that even though progress seems slow or non-existent at times, there is a plan that is being followed.

Timely Counseling

"Structuring" is the technical term professional counselors use to define the nature, limits, and goals of the counseling process. Part of structuring includes determining not only an overall goal but also time limits. For pastors, this part of structuring is absolutely crucial — their demanding schedule will be overwhelmed otherwise.

Setting time limits begins with setting the limits of the counseling unit. The fifty-minute hour has evolved as the standard. In less than half an hour you can hardly get caught up. In longer than fifty minutes, there's usually overload.

While we may feel awkward about cutting a needy person off after fifty minutes (it seems too sterile, hardly pastoral), the extra minutes requested often turn into an hour. If that happens just a couple of times, then other responsibilities quickly get shortchanged.

We also need to remember that most of the healing in therapy takes place not in the session but between sessions. Between sessions the person reflects on what's been said. The session is actually only a boost, an energizer in the healing process.

If you spend too much time in counseling, you run the risk of interfering with a normal healing process. If you give too much antibiotic, you're not only going to kill the germs, you're going to kill a whole bunch of healthy organisms as well.

Besides setting limits on each session, long-term counselors should determine how long they'll see a particular person. Usually it's unwise to commit yourself for longer than six months. You may, in fact, think that the problem will require a year or two, but you don't announce that to a counselee. That not only could discourage a counselee, it commits the pastor to a term of counseling that may be unrealistic.

As part of that decision, you have to determine how often you'll meet — once a week, every other week, or once a month — as well as the specific appointment: "Let's meet each Tuesday afternoon at three o'clock."

In fact, the pastor should have clearly defined times of the week when counseling takes place. To counsel on the run, to respond only when someone needs it is not good long-term practice. It undermines your ability to give quality counseling. And frankly, it wears the counselor out. Counseling is demanding enough without the added burden of haphazard scheduling.

What Does Progress Look Like?

In long-term counseling we aim for a change in the person's basic beliefs, lifestyle, or personality. Such change takes place very slowly, and sometimes it's hard to see much progress. If we recognize what types of changes ought to be taking place in each stage of long-term counseling, we are in a better position to determine if the counselee is making progress.

● *Early stage.* In the early stage the goal is to get through the outer defense system. Even people who come for counseling are reluctant to share who they are. Their early confessions are superficial. I've worked with people who couldn't trust me with intimate knowledge about themselves even after six months of counseling.

One test I use when working with pastors is to ask, "Tell me a little about your sexuality." Until they trust me, they'll change the subject. That is not frustrating to me, but it is a sign that I haven't reached the goal in the first stage of long-term therapy.

● *Middle stage.* You know you're in the middle stages when people start sharing deeper concerns. Embarrassing things, almost shameful things begin to emerge. And so there's a sense of progress as one moves deeper into the inner world of that person; they begin to trust you more with the private thoughts, even fantasies.

After coming to me for six months, one pastor finally began telling me that he had strong homosexual feelings. He was married, had a lovely family, had never been near a gay man, but all his fantasies were of men.

Once a person has opened himself in this way, I may think that's an open invitation to explore further. If I go too fast, however, I will encounter resistance, either in the form of changing the subject or in defensive anger.

In this stage, the man who was domineering toward his wife finally began sharing with me his sexual fantasies, and they were fantasies of abuse and flogging. If, in fact, this was a way of getting back at his domineering mother, and if I had pushed and asked, "Is this a way to get back at your mother for domineering you?" I might have gotten an angry denial: "Whatever gave you that idea! I would never dream of hurting my mother!" That would have set the counseling back. I need to be sensitive to the pace of revelation that the counselee wants to set.

I can cause even more resistance if I respond to the anger at a level the counselee is not ready to accept. If the next week I say, "Why did you get angry last week?" he may respond with denial: "What do you mean? I wasn't angry." The man may still not be willing to accept the emotions about his mother that are swirling within him.

I need to explore the anger, but I've found it better to tone down the question to a level of understanding people are usually ready to deal with: "To me you seemed upset last week. What do you think was going on?"

Then they are more able to process it: "Well, I don't think so. But let me think about it. You could be right."

● *Final stage.* In the final stage, the counselor and client begin to pull together in a meaningful way the information and insights that have emerged. The client now begins to see connections, how decisions and actions lead to consequences and how those consequences can be avoided if she makes the right decisions.

The domineering man who had abusive sexual fantasies began to realize, *If I didn't go to the porno shop so much, maybe if I just stopped exposing myself to that stuff, it wouldn't hook me as much. Maybe if I stopped viewing women being abused, I could start seeing my wife in a different light.*

In this stage, the counselor suggests courses of action to speed the healing. To the woman who had stolen from her parents, I recommended she make restitution: for her deceased parents we had to go through a little ritual, asking parental forgiveness; for her remaining sister, she shared some of her inheritance and reestablished a relationship with her.

When There Are No Signs of Progress

Some problems, like histrionic disorders, will heal very slowly. It doesn't surprise me if I go a year or two with little progress. With sexual disorders, on the other hand, if I don't see progress in a matter of five or six weeks, I become concerned. So the nature of the problem determines what "progress" means.

No matter the problem, though, I sometimes feel as if clients are not progressing. In some cases, I'm right: they've repeatedly resisted my probing into their deeper motives — in some cases it's because they hold religious beliefs that get in the way of healing (for example, one man believed that unless his offender repented and asked his and God's forgiveness, the person wasn't entitled to his forgiveness).

When people keep on resisting progress, as I conclude a session I'll tell them, "For the last ten minutes of the session I would like to find out where you're coming from. I feel there has not been a lot of progress these last three months, that we have skirted around some issues. And issues that interest you seem to have no relationship to our larger goal. How are you feeling about the process? Do you think we've done enough? Is it time to stop coming to me?"

That usually alerts them to the fact they need to keep working. And for those who really don't want to work, it gives them a gracious out.

In the case of the woman I counseled for ten years, I tried to terminate with her several times from year five to year eight. But every time I tried to terminate, she objected strongly. She was convinced things were getting better. She felt hopeful the process would bring some major outcome. So I stuck with her.

Often, though, I don't see progress because I'm unable to see what's going on deep inside an individual. That a counselee still comes, of course, is a signal he or she wants to change. Still, I find it helpful periodically to check in with the client, simply asking if we are making any progress, using such questions as: "How are we doing?" "Is this doing you any good?" "What benefits are you gaining?" and "Where do you think we ought to be going?"

Terminating the Therapy

Termination is the process by which the counselor helps the client summarize what's happened in the counseling, highlight the main insights, point to progress, plan for the near future, and end the counseling relationship. This can take one session, or up to six months.

A danger in this stage is to terminate prematurely. Because of the demands on my time and the number of people who want to see me, I'm often tempted to end things abruptly. I sometimes think people are ready to move on before they are ready. When I do push them out too quickly, though, I provoke a crisis.

I might say to a counselee, "I don't think I'll need to see you for a while. I think we're done; we've accomplished what we set out to accomplish."

She walks out on cloud nine, full of self-confidence. For a day or two she feels great, and then she begins to feel abandoned. She's afraid; she feels alone.

And that's when I get a cry for help: a phone call in the middle of the night; she's in tears, begging to see me. Sometimes people feel they have to exaggerate their pathology to get the counselor's attention again. Naturally, I need to bring such people back in and keep working with them.

Then again, some people resist termination because they've become dependent on the counselor. They can't make decisions without checking with the counselor. The counselor becomes substitute husband, father, parent, lover. And the longer the counseling, the more transference develops.

Counseling is never done, however, until the transference is resolved. You cannot terminate long-term counseling in the middle of a transference.

If I try to terminate a counseling relationship while the person is highly dependent on me, the counselee will kick up a fuss: "I'm not ready to quit!"

So I'll ask, "Well how much longer do you think it would be appropriate for us to counsel?"

If the response is something like, "Well, I'm not thinking of any limit right now" or "Another six months," then I continue. I must help the counselee work through the dependence before terminating.

I receive a Christmas card each year from the woman I counseled for over ten years. And each year, I am reminded of the challenges and rewards of long-term counseling. It requires tremendous patience, much more than I often have, and forces me to hear some pretty messy stuff that goes on deep in people's lives.

But long-term counseling also gives me the unparalleled opportunity to witness firsthand the subtle yet powerful healing that God brings. I feel I am collaborating with God's Spirit, who over time convicts and enlightens and guides the people I'm working with, bringing them to full mental, emotional, and spiritual health.

The differences between men and women are usually subtle and often don't follow a stereotyped pattern. Then again, there's a reason for the stereotypes and a reason for counselors to know them.

— *Jim Smith*

CHAPTER EIGHT
Counseling Men, Counseling Women

*H*e gave *her* a pair of shock absorbers for her birthday. She wasn't happy. She came to see me, dragging her husband behind.

"He's so insensitive," she complained about her husband. "He doesn't really care about me. He never thinks about what I want. What made him think I would want shock absorbers for my birthday? I sometimes wonder if he even loves me."

He couldn't understand the problem. "Heck, she's been complaining about the bouncy ride in the car. And our car was unsafe with the old shock absorbers. I thought she'd appreciate the fact that I'm watching out for her comfort and safety."

This brief, somewhat humorous composite of countless counseling experiences displays many of the dynamics that take place in counseling men and women. These dynamics are essential for me to understand. If I know how men usually act and how women usually act, I know better what to listen for and how to respond effectively.

Identifying the differences between men and women can help in many counseling situations. The differences are subtle, and not always do they follow a stereotyped pattern. Then again, there's a reason for the stereotypes and a reason for us to know them.

It's like Jose Canseco's knowing that Nolan Ryan usually throws a fastball on a three-and-two count. It's helpful in most of those situations, although Canseco also needs to be prepared for a hard curve.

Most men and most women fall into certain psychological patterns. Although many will throw us hard curves, understanding their usual patterns of behavior can enhance our ability to successfully counsel them.

Differences that Make a Difference

First, we need to explore some of the usual differences that men and women bring into our offices.

• *Talking heads and silent Sams.* Women usually volunteer more information than you need, men less than you would like.

In fact, we may find ourselves feeling verbally overwhelmed by a woman who elaborates in great detail about her troubles.

For example, one woman who came to me started out like a machine gun. She didn't cease from the moment she walked in. I thought, *This woman has to breathe some time. I'm going to catch her when she does!* But I never spotted a pause during the fifty minutes. She unloaded so many details, I lost track of what she was saying.

Some women will run down a rabbit trail of thought, and then another, and then another, before finally getting back on course. Others will burst in with, "Oh, you just wouldn't believe what I've gotten myself into. I'm so disappointed in myself. I know the Lord's mad at me and never going to love me again. I don't know how I let myself . . ." talking for ten minutes about I-don't-know-what.

At that point I'll often say, "Time out. Hold on. Tell me what you're talking about." But I usually don't have to say much more than that to get them to talk in detail about what's going on.

On the other hand, with men I often have to prime the pump in order to get a clear idea of what's going on.

A man will sit down and say, "I don't know how to get started . . . I don't know where to begin . . . I'm embarrassed to be here . . . I don't know why I came . . . This is hard for me . . . I'm involved with a woman."

"Well, tell me about it."

"Well, I just did."

With men I often have to probe with specific questions to find out the scope of their problem: "What's this woman's name? Where did you meet her? What attracted you to her?"

● *Careers and relationships.* Men tend to wrestle more with problems in their career and less with problems at home. In fact, a man can tolerate a fairly low degree of marital happiness if his career is moving forward.

Women cannot. They tend to struggle more with relationships. And that's why women seek marital counseling much more often than men. They've got more eggs in the relational basket.

Many women today grapple with dual career issues, especially how much time they should give the family. They feel they neglect the family if they pursue an outside job.

A typical man says, "My job is to earn the bread, and my wife's is to run the home." A typical woman, even if she's pursuing a career, still feels she's primarily responsible for relationships at home.

I counsel many single women who avidly pursue their careers and who are simply miserable. They say, "If I can just get married, it would solve all my problems," or "My relationships with men don't go well. I date a guy for six months, and then he just drops off the face of the earth."

Even single women, then, are more concerned about relation-ships. I have very few women who say to me, "I've got a financial crisis" or "My business is about to go under; can we talk?"

● *Expectations of counseling.* Women tend to come for counsel-ing earlier in their problem. They seek help more quickly. Men don't like to admit they need help. Just as men balk at stopping and asking for directions — we hate to admit we don't have control of a situation — men are more prideful and therefore more reluctant to come for counseling.

But when men do come in, they expect a solution, a report: "Give me a game plan to address this. I want to leave here having a better grasp on my options."

Women usually come in wanting support: "I want somebody to understand me." So the ministry of presence is a lot more impor-tant with women. The ministry of providing options is more impor-tant for men.

● *Fears in counseling.* Many men are afraid they're going to break down emotionally during counseling. When men cry in ses-sions, they usually apologize. Every man who has cried in my office has been embarrassed about it.

We go through a lot more boxes of Kleenex with women than with men. And although women often cry, they seldom apologize for it. They may begin by saying, "Well, I was determined not to cry when I came in here" but conclude, "but I'm going to cry."

On the other hand, women are afraid that I'm not going to think well of them if they tell me some dark fantasy or secret or urge. They feel they will be considered unworthy of my ministry: "You're going to reject me if I tell you this," they'll say.

Men aren't so concerned about sharing their transgressions or fantasies. They'll typically say, "I'm not proud of this, but I think about my friend's wife a lot."

Then again, men are more embarrassed by failures, particularly in business or in supporting their families. That bothers them more than sexual infidelity. It would be the opposite for most women.

• *Personality tendencies.* I like to think of mental health as a continuum: to the left are people who feel excessively responsible for others (neurotics) and to the right people who are too wrapped up in themselves (narcissists). On this continuum, women tend to fall on the left and men to the right.

People on the extreme left are excessively guilty. They take far more responsibility for things than they ought to take. They step on an ant and can't sleep at night.

One woman came in and told me she was feeling guilty because she had hung up the phone when her mother called. In the course of the conversation, I discovered that it had been the tenth time that day that her mother had called.

The woman said, "You know, I really ought to be more sensitive to my mother. She gave her life for me and risked life bringing me into the world, and yet I got so mad at her and hung up. I'm so embarrassed and ashamed."

Or, take a woman whose husband has had half a dozen affairs who says, "I know I'm doing something wrong in the marriage. I'm just not meeting his needs."

That's excessively neurotic.

A milder version of excessive neurosis is co-dependency, which I also see in many more women than men.

On the right of the continuum we find most men. They are, in general, narcissists: people who believe the world exists to serve them. They are self-absorbed. Narcissus was a figure in Greek mythology who was always looking at his own reflection. Men are not necessarily vain, just self-absorbed.

In the extreme, this type of man thinks of his wife as something he hangs on his arm to show off in the business world. Or, he might reason, the kids can't have new shoes, but he's going to have a Rolex watch, because, after all, in the business world you've got to dress for success.

A married couple who were in debt $100,000 to credit cards came to see me. After the first session I asked them to draw up a budget. The next week they returned, but the wife was sheepish.

"I'm embarrassed," she said.

"I understand that," I replied. "But we need to look at the figures to come up with a financial plan for you."

After we worked through one year's budget, there was still $40,000 unaccounted for. When I asked about it, they became even more sheepish.

"What did you do?" I asked.

"Well, we took a few vacations."

"How many is a few?"

"Four."

"You blew $40,000 on vacations when you had $100,000 debt to credit cards?" I said.

"Well, you know, I've been busting my tail," the man said, "and I thought we deserved it."

That's narcissism.

Narcissists also tend to be more insensitive to their own sins and their own collusion in events. When he is caught, let's say stealing money from his employer, he will be more embarrassed that he got caught than that he committed a sin against society: "This will ruin my reputation!" When the narcissist has an affair, he thinks less about betrayal of his marriage vows and how he's hurt his wife and more about what people will think if it gets out.

Of course, most men are not this extreme, but their tendency toward narcissism is clear.

These are but a few of the generalizations about men and women that hold true. To nuance this a bit, let me draw out one aspect of working with men and one with women that will help us understand our relationship with each of them a little better still.

Men: Occupation Isn't Always Everything

What I've said about men doesn't hold true for all, nor does it hold true forever. There comes a time when their preoccupation with occupation and their own reflection shifts dramatically. Counselors are wise to note it.

Up to age 40, men focus on their careers. They're nearly consumed with long-term goals, career achievement. Men under 40 who come to see me are usually struggling with work-related issues: they've not gotten a promotion, been transferred, or been laid off. Much of their self-esteem is wrapped up in their work.

When a man hits his mid-forties, a shift takes place. By the time we're 45 we've either attained our occupational goals or, usually, we haven't and are not going to. And men have to come to terms with that. This, of course, is the classic mid-life crisis when many men decide to shape their lives differently.

One shift is that men in their forties start to get in touch with their emotions and their relationships. They are ready to give themselves to their kids. The problem is that just when the father has more time and energy to give to his kids, the kids are in their late teens, saying "Hey, I'm out of here" or "Where were you when I really needed you?"

The man may also try to build new bridges to his wife, with varying degrees of success, depending on how stable their marriage has been.

This is also a time when men get in touch with their mortality. A 20-year-old man thinks he's bulletproof. By the time men hit their forties, they start hearing about friends and business acquaintances who have had heart attacks or contracted fatal diseases. So men will come in to deal with the fact that they are not going to live forever, and often that puts them on a spiritual quest.

This period in a man's life is critical for the counselor to be aware of.

Women: Emotional Seduction

It's not unusual for a woman client to become sexually attracted to her pastor/counselor. What many pastors fail to see, however, is that they, the pastors, often encourage this, albeit unintentionally.

The pastor is always understanding towards the woman: he is present when she needs him, seems to understand everything she feels, and never confronts her. It doesn't take long before she starts comparing him with her husband: "Why am I married to this clod when I have a wonderful, sensitive, caring, loving, concerned person like my pastor?"

That's when the woman becomes emotionally seduced. There's nothing sexual about it yet. The problem is, once a woman is emotionally seduced, she is subject to falling in love and then being sexually attracted to the pastor.

In the meantime, the pastor has simply been doing a good job at counseling, and this is the result.

The way to avoid emotional seduction is first to be aware of the power our caring demeanor has over women. It's the very thing that many of them crave in a man. When we give our care, as we should, we need to be aware of what it can do to a woman.

Second, we need to make sure that emotional expressions on our part are not subject to misinterpretation.

Take touching, for instance. I rarely do it. About the only time I ever touch a woman is when I pray with her; I may take her hand while I pray. Also, when a woman looks horribly in the dumps, I might say, "You look like you could use a hug. Would you like a hug?" And if she agrees, and only then, I'll do it. But even then, I won't do a full frontal embrace or a long squeeze — just a gentle hug, one arm around the shoulder. I want to offer comfort, but I don't want even to imply anything else.

When a woman client asks me for a hug, I have to make a judgment. If I'm at all concerned that it would be inappropriate, I'll defer, but so as not to offend: "Tell me what's happening. Why is that important to you right now?"

During a session, some women try to get physically closer to me than I'm comfortable with. In such cases I'll say, "I sense that you prefer to be closer to me than the chairs are normally arranged. I wonder if we can talk about why that is important to you."

Such phrases are powerful at diffusing potentially troubling situations. I use them often.

Often the borderline personalities are those who can be the

most troublesome in this regard. A pastor should be able to recognize such a person, especially a female borderline. Here are a few of the more recognizable traits:

● Alternates between extremes of idolizing the counselor and then despising him.

● Impulsive in at least two areas that are potentially self-damaging, i.e., spending, sex, substance use, shoplifting, reckless driving, binge eating.

● Frequent displays of temper, constant anger, recurrent physical fights.

● Recurrent suicidal threats or gestures, or self-mutilating behavior.

● Chronic feelings of emptiness or boredom.

● Frantic efforts to avoid real or imagined abandonment.

Almost all borderline women were abandoned early in their lives, have emotionally distant fathers, or were sexually abused by fathers.

The problem is that most pastors, as males, tend toward narcissism. And it's the combination of the borderline ("Pastor, you're great; you're the one who can really help me") and the narcissist ("Finally, somebody sees how gifted I am; here's someone whom I can really help") that can be explosive. A lot of the sexual indiscretion in the pastorate has its source in this combination.

At the same time, the pastor who refuses to be manipulated by the borderline can find himself in deep trouble as well. If the borderline feels rejected, she lashes back, perhaps starting false rumors that the pastor is cold and aloof, or worse, that the pastor has committed adultery. Or she'll approach the pastor after the service and give him a suggestive squeeze, as one did to me. Borderlines can be extremely sinister.

That's all the more reason to establish clear safeguards and boundaries in the counseling session. Never go to a woman's home or apartment alone. Never counsel in your office without another person being in the building.

And if I hear about rumors, I try to deal with them as quickly and gently as I can. One borderline whom I had been seeing said she thought I was having an affair with a female staff member of the church. I responded, "Let's talk about that. What makes you think that? Why do you feel that way?" That often settles things down quickly.

But working with borderlines is a tricky business. It's a mine-field for pastors, as it is for doctors, politicians, and lawyers.

Temporary Father

One more important difference to note: To many men and women I become the father they lost at an early age or the loving person their father wasn't. To a limited extent that's a legitimate transference. And how specifically that works itself out with women and with men is different.

● *Male authority figure.* Many women come to me to experience some of the parental strokes they did not get or can no longer get from their fathers.

A woman came in recently, and she cried and cried. "My father died,' she sobbed, "and you're the only man I can talk to." So I became a replacement figure for her father.

And that was okay for a while. I eventually had to deal with the transference; I didn't want to get hooked into becoming the answer man for her for the rest of her life. I wanted to help her have enough confidence in her own ability to deal with life without a male authority figure. But first I had to make sure her immediate emotional needs were met. Only then would she be able to step back and get a new perspective.

In such a situation, when the right moment comes, perhaps two or three sessions later, I'll say, "Are you aware of the power you've given me, over how I feel about what you do and think? Is that something you want to continue to do all of your life?" Or I'll say, "It seems to me that how you feel about your decisions is based on whether I approve of them or not."

Pastors have to be especially careful with sexually abused women. A lot of them have been abused by their fathers or important male figures. So we need to build relationships without being exploitive or abusive

I once counseled a woman whose father repeatedly told her how ugly she was. Actually, she's a very attractive woman. And yet all her life she has been hearing that other message. As a counselor, I had to act as a "new father," not so she could become dependent on me, but so she could hear some affirmation from a male authority figure.

Naturally, I had to be careful how I did that — I didn't want it to appear as a come on. So at a socially safe physical distance and in a matter-of-fact tone of voice, I said something like, "You know, as a man, I don't experience you that way. I don't see you as ugly. I see you as an attractive woman."

I didn't move close to her at that time. I didn't say, "Boy, you really look good today. Wow, you've really got a nice figure!" All that would have been suggestive.

And once she began to have some emotional equilibrium, I tried to get her to see that she could feel good about herself regardless of what her father or I said.

● *Male confidant.* For many men, I become the father whom they could never talk with. Perhaps their father was never emotionally available, either too busy or too cold. Perhaps their father never gave them permission to fail, or perhaps their father deserted them. In any case, the best thing I can do for such men is to become a non-threatening, safe confidant.

In fact, I've had dozens of men over the years tell me, "You're the only man I can talk to about this." It's a disturbing truth.

Naturally, I try to help these men learn to confide in other men. But first, they need to build up some confidence and trust by confiding in me, treating me as a father figure.

There are some men, of course, who need to deal with a mother figure for a while. Perhaps their mother was domineering and controlling, and it's affecting them still. They need to experience an affirming relationship with a woman therapist. So I'll refer such men.

Counseling Each

If men and women have these differences, it only makes sense that in many instances I will counsel them differently. Here is one way I approach each.

● *Women: feelings before thoughts.* Many women cannot think about their options, about what they ought to do, until they have first worked through their feelings about a matter. For women, it's feelings first, thoughts second.

An airline attendant and her husband were having difficulties — in fact, he had had an affair, and the mistress had killed herself. If that wasn't bad enough, without telling his wife, he had quit his job and taken a new position in Alaska, and he expected her to quit the airlines to come along.

When she came in to see me, she was livid, and I just let her rage about all that her husband had done to her: "You just can't believe what my husband has done to me. I hate the bastard!" When she had fumed and ranted for some time, she started to settle down.

After discussing her feelings for a while, I finally said, "I sure understand how you feel. So, what are your thoughts about the marriage?"

"Well, I want to make it work," she said. And we proceeded to reframe the issue. For example, when we talked about the job move, I said, "I can certainly see how you feel about the unexpected move. But it's possible that he simply wants to be a more conscientious provider, and here was an opportunity to provide almost triple what he was making. It may not have occurred to him that you would not agree with his decision. There may be no malice on his part, just thoughtlessness."

At that point, she was ready to see things from another perspective, beyond her hurt. If I had confronted her at the beginning of the session with "Are you going to make this work or not?" we wouldn't have gotten anywhere. I had to hold off from analysis until I fully understood the complexity and depth of the woman's feelings. Once she felt supported and affirmed, then she was ready to deal with solutions.

● *Men: thoughts before feelings.* As I mentioned, men come

expecting a solution or game plan as a result of counseling. They're ready to analyze as soon as they step in the door. But for a healthy solution to come about, they too need to process their feelings. But with men, I have to put feelings on hold until we've had a chance to get their thoughts on the table.

When this man who had committed adultery and changed jobs came in to talk, we spent the first part of the session just talking about what had happened. I asked him questions like, "Tell me about how you met her. What did she mean to you? What were your experiences with her? Tell me about the last time you were with her."

Then we talked about what he planned to do.

"Well, the woman's family is coming to town to claim the body, and I'm going to meet them at the apartment. I've got to tell my wife, because she's not going to understand. . . ."

All this talk about what had happened and what he was going to do was his systematic way of avoiding the pain. But after he had talked for a while, I said, "My guess is this has been pretty painful to you. How do you feel about her killing herself?"

And then the gusher opened up, and he was able to talk about that: "I'm feeling pretty guilty. I feel I was responsible. . . ."

My guess is he would not have immediately revealed that. First, we had to talk about thoughts.

The depth of the differences between men and women is profound. I've just sketched a few fundamental differences here and how I deal with them. Counselees, of course, constantly throw me curveballs: a woman will come in consumed with her career, a man will want to immediately explore his own feelings.

But most of the time I see the fastballs I expect. And knowing that they'll be coming has helped me be a better counselor for men and for women.

Every problem has a context, and to solve a problem we often have to work on the context.

— Archibald Hart

CHAPTER NINE
All in the Family

Until she turned fifty, Marjorie had been an "ideal" housewife and mother. She had without complaint sacrificed her needs to move with her husband to the country so he could set up shop as a lawyer in a small town. She had raised a daughter to the conservative standards of their town. She was faithful in attendance at church and the women's group and regularly volunteered for Sunday school duty.

When she turned fifty, though, she began to wonder if life wasn't passing her by. She became lethargic. She thought her life dull and meaningless and without hope. She became severely depressed. She talked of suicide.

That's when she came to see me. She remained depressed until her 17-year-old daughter began dating, weekly going out drinking and dancing in a nearby city.

Suddenly the mother came out of her depression: she started dressing like a teenager and mimicking her daughter — much to her daughter's embarrassment. The daughter got angry, and the next thing I discovered was that the daughter became pregnant.

Somehow most of this was kept from the busy husband. But when he discovered what had been going on, he became extremely depressed himself. He tried to placate his wife and keep her out of the view of the townspeople, setting her up in a separate apartment in the city.

What's the problem here? Partly, it's the wife. She just could not handle aging. She had never come to terms with getting old.

But had I counseled this woman as if she were the problem, I would have missed the larger dynamic.

After bringing the husband and daughter into counseling, I realized the wife had, with the husband's prodding, become deeply enmeshed in her husband's work: she entertained his clients, she kept up appearances to increase his business. She had started to become the model lawyer's wife and had no life of her own. Now she was rebelling. She didn't want anything to do with his work or life.

Her husband had never allowed her to work outside the home, so she had never earned her own money; she had never bought anything for herself without her husband's approval. In addition to turning fifty, she was pulling away from the family system that had been oppressing her for so long.

The father had also excessively controlled the life of his daughter, and the daughter was rebelling against that.

I realized that we had to work on how the family interacted before I was going to make any progress with the wife's regression to adolescent behavior.

We started to make some progress, but not without bumping into a few hurdles. The daughter had her baby. She didn't want to marry the young man who fathered the child, but neither did she want to give up the baby for adoption.

During this time, the father had given up his law practice to please his wife. But he had difficulty at first finding another job. So we had to work through all these other adjustments as well.

Every Problem Has a Context

Marjorie's problem may be extreme, but it illustrates the fact that every problem has a context and that to solve a problem we often have to work on this same context.

I could have taken an individualistic approach: "Marjorie, you've just got to accept that you are getting older. Let's work on this together." That would not have addressed some deeper issues in her life.

I could have set her free from her oppressive context: "There's no reason for you to stick around with such a husband. He's married to his work. Your husband is your problem. You need to find yourself." By now she would have been divorced, living alone, and playing the field, feeling miserable and lonely.

To address Marjorie's larger situation complicated the counseling process immensely. Instead of dealing with one person, I had to think about six relationships (the three among them, and me with each). Instead of addressing one problem, I had to address many.

But it was well worth the extra effort. It produced a larger good than simply helping Marjorie deal with aging. I was able to help a family live together in a healthier way for years to come.

As the Bible teaches: God has designed us to live in relationships. I've found that true in my counseling experience — no one has an individual problem that doesn't in some way affect the family and isn't in some way affected by the family. So when it becomes clear that the issue under discussion seriously affects family dynamics, I try to involve members of the family in the counseling process. Here are some guidelines I follow.

When to Take Family Cases

When a pastor discovers that a problem goes deeper than the counselee and that others should be brought in, it doesn't necessarily mean he or she should immediately begin counseling the family. It depends, of course, on the pastor's expertise, but in general, some of these cases are better referred to a professional specialist.

For example, if the family problem is deeply rooted — it has gone on for a generation or more, it has biological roots, or a family member has a serious personality disorder — then most pastors are wise to make a referral.

I worked with one woman who was clearly manic depressive. Stress will bring this pathology out, but biology is clearly part of its roots. She responded to the medication I recommended, but she had three daughters, two of whom had inherited the same manic and depressive tendency. Though in their late twenties, they were still living at home. The whole family system was contaminated with a fairly serious mental and emotional illness that had a biological root. This is clearly a case a pastor should refer to a professional psychiatrist.

Then again, some family cases are more appropriate for a pastor to take, even more appropriate than for a psychologist or psychiatrist. For example, when a family is causing a person deep psychological stress but refuses to become part of the person's healing, that's when a pastor can be a great help.

If a professional counselor goes to the person's family members and says, "I need to see other members of the family to really be of help to So-and-so," the family is likely to respond, "You're exaggerating the problem just to get more clients and more fees in your pocket."

The pastor is one of the few professionals who can seek out and encourage a family to get help without raising suspicions about motives. There's nothing in it for the pastor but time and effort. If the pastor shows that effort, it often convinces the family to seek out help.

If the problems of counselee and family are moral in nature or require reconciliation and forgiveness, then a pastor, as representative of the one who reconciles heaven and earth, is usually the better person to draw the family into counseling. Generally, reconciliation and forgiveness is more powerfully and effectively handled by a pastoral counselor than by a professional counselor. Such issues are more spiritual than psychological in nature.

Don't Believe Everything You Hear

A woman comes in depressed: "My problem is my husband. He doesn't give me attention. He's not affectionate enough. He's not interested in me as a woman anymore."

Or a man says, "My kids are such a pain to me. They just want everything I can give them. They show me no respect."

It may be true that some family dynamic ought to change, but it's also true that people are rarely mere victims of other people's behavior.

In fact, in the last few years, I've begun to realize that many people who come to see me, although they appear to be the victims of a bad system, are often victimizers of that system. Sometimes they're the ones causing most of the problems at home, and they've come to me to help them change their families, but they do not understand their contribution to the problem. The counselor easily gets caught in the trap of seeing the problem only from the counselee's point of view, forming a therapeutic alliance with the counselee against the family.

I guard against this by bringing in all the family members involved as soon as I see some larger dynamics. And when I do bring them in, I try to see the issue from the family's point of view. That's when I often discover that my counselee is more a victimizer than a victim.

If counselors aren't careful to seek out the whole truth before applying therapy, the outcome can be less than ideal.

In one local case, a daughter alleged that her father had sexually abused her. The therapist, believing that the daughter had no reason to lie, wanted to perform an intervention and conspired to confront the father in front of other family members. The counselor and the daughter convinced the whole family of her accusations.

So without knowing what was going on, the father was confronted by the therapist and family about an alleged sexual abuse. He was devastated, and that's when I was brought in.

However, in talking with the daughter, I immediately suspected that no such abuse actually took place. The daughter was a seriously disturbed woman. I discovered that the therapist had not thoroughly evaluated her mental condition and had misjudged her honesty. It became evident to everyone that there was no truth whatsoever in her accusations. It was all a fabrication of a very troubled mind.

Studies have shown that one out of three children who report abuse from their parents distort the truth. Counselors have to be careful about believing everything they hear. In any case, I always seek to understand the real dynamics of a family before suggesting any action.

The beauty of counseling people in context is this: I'm not caught up in forming an alliance with the counselee against the rest of the world; I'm more concerned about discovering the truthfulness of what is going on. And I tell people this up front when they come to see me. It keeps deception to a minimum.

Avoid Getting "Triangled"

I get "triangled" when I and the counselee try together to solve the problem of a third party.

For example, a woman with an alcoholic husband tells me "I've tried everything. I'm at the end of my rope. I don't know what to do. Can you help me get my husband to stop drinking?"

An empathetic counselor will have a hard time not biting on the bait: "Let's see what we can do. Try this first: You go home and pour all his liquor down the drain. Then tell him you won't give him sex until he quits."

At that point, I've become triangled: the wife and I have ganged up on the husband and together are going to change him.

The problem is, once a counselor does that, the third party reacts violently. The husband feels like he's being ganged up on, and he is. The counselor is likely to become the enemy and the therapeutic relationship destroyed: "That pastor you're seeing is just causing problems. I don't want you seeing him anymore if this is what's going to happen." Now there is more conflict than ever in the marriage. The counselor has become triangled.

The mistake here is for counselors to think they can change the third dimension of a triangle. We cannot solve the man's drinking problem directly or fix the relationship between the husband and wife. We do not have direct access to the husband; nor has he asked for help.

We can, though, maintain clearly "differentiated" relationships with the wife and with the husband, nurturing separate relationships with each, helping each figure out what he or she should do to heal the situation. But we shouldn't try to heal it for them.

I can change only a relationship of which I am a part. I can't deal with the alcoholism. I can only build a relationship. So I must endeavor to build a relationship with the alcoholic husband directly. Only then can I influence the alcoholic husband.

So instead I would say to the wife, "I see that your husband's drinking is causing you a great deal of stress. I can't, however, tell you what you should do to help him stop drinking. You'll have to work that out with him yourself. But I can help you deal with your stress and help you figure out things you can do to help your husband."

If I'm able to convince the husband to see me, I could ask him about his drinking, if he thinks it's a problem, what he thinks his wife's concern is, and so on.

If the husband refuses to recognize the problem, then I must simply support the wife by encouraging her and helping her react appropriately. But I don't work through her to change the alcoholic husband. I work at strengthening my relationship with her.

(If the man is dangerous or if he's abusing her, then the matter becomes a legal issue, and I have no choice but to intervene by reporting it to the appropriate authorities.)

If the husband refuses to acknowledge his problem, the pastor-counselor is in an advantageous position when compared to the professional counselor. A pastor can make friendly calls to the home. He or she can drop off notes or make phone calls — expected behavior from a pastor. The pastor can foster a natural relationship that could develop into a therapeutic relationship.

The Place of Interventions

One of the options a counselor could give such a wife is to encourage her to organize an intervention with her husband. Still, it must be her decision to go ahead, and she must be willing to live with the consequences.

The counselor could be intricately involved in preparing the intervention. Perhaps the key role the counselor plays is making sure the family that gathers to confront the husband will not undermine the intervention with their own discord.

A pastor friend once called me about his alcoholic father. "My brother is going to be in town for a couple of days, and I'm thinking of setting up a family intervention with my dad. My brother thinks I'm rushing things. What do you think?"

"That would be foolish," I replied bluntly. "Among other reasons, your family needs to convene a couple of times to plan a strategy before meeting with your father. You all need to talk through your feelings about your father's alcoholism to make sure you agree about the strategy. Otherwise you could begin the intervention and find some members of the family starting to feel sorry for your father; they'll begin taking sides, and soon the intervention could disintegrate.

"You also need to know how to respond to the reactions that occur in such an intervention. Only when your family is prepared to counteract your father's possible responses and are in total agreement will your saying to your father, 'You've got to get help,' do any good."

Don't Keep Secrets

One extremely important rule should guide all family counseling: No secrets. That is, no forming an alliance with another with the express purpose of deceiving a third party.

To hark back to the opening story, when the daughter discovered she was pregnant, the mother's first reaction to me was, "We've got to keep this secret. We've got to keep it from my husband. We've got to keep it from the town, especially from our church."

I immediately responded, "No. No secrets."

"Well," she said, "Then you tell my husband."

"No, that's not my responsibility. Let's figure out a way you or your daughter can tell your husband."

We talked it over and finally decided that the daughter must tell her father. And although the father and daughter were in severe conflict, she told him. In the end, though, the daughter and the father discovered a new relationship with each other. A tremendous bonding occurred.

If, however, the mother and daughter had waited three months to tell the father, and if he had found out from another source, it would have been disastrous. He would have felt violated, and the relationship could have been worsened for years.

There's a difference, of course, between confidentiality and secrets. I kept the information about the daughter in confidence. The counselor doesn't break confidences. So I wouldn't have said a thing about it.

If the father had asked me directly about it: "There's a rumor going around about my daughter being pregnant. You've been seeing her and my wife. Is it true?" I would have replied, "Whether it's true or not, I can't comment. What goes on in the counseling session is confidential. If you want to know something about your daughter, you better talk with her." And I would have continued to urge the daughter and mother to talk to the father.

Certainly there are judgment calls. A woman troubled about an abortion she had a decade earlier while in another relationship probably isn't required to tell her husband of eight years. A man habitually addicted to pornography should certainly tell his wife. But many cases lie about halfway between these extremes.

Sometimes the information shared would, in fact, do more harm than good. I've counseled married men who've confessed homosexual fantasies. I've not encouraged them to share those with their wives, it would put an unfair burden on them.

Sometimes groundwork must be done before information is shared. A husband has a one-night stand and wants to confess it to his wife. I usually ask the husband to remain faithful to his wife for a year or two, improve his relationship with her, show her by his actions that she is the most important woman in his life. Then both are in a better position when he confesses.

Although there are exceptions, then, my usual course is strongly to encourage clients to tell their loved ones any information that bears directly on their present relationship. At a minimum this includes telling their important loved ones that they are getting counseling.

Two Cautions

As I begin working with families, I stay aware of two dangers.

● *Sabotage.* Families develop patterns of responding to their problems. Homeostasis develops; a level of psychological equilibrium is found that helps keep the peace in relationships. Each person finds his or her level of involvement and balance with each other person. Everyone finds a role.

So families are reluctant to change their system of interacting, even if it's causing one person great stress. In fact, family systems are far more difficult to change than individuals. The more you try to change the system, the more stress the system causes.

A family system is a much more complex organism to work with than an individual. Individuals are complex enough; but multiply that two, three, four, five times, and now you have tremendous complexity. So, families are fraught with dynamics that cannot always be understood or differentiated.

And if you push families too hard for change, they are likely to sabotage the healing process: "Ever since this counselor started working with us, we've had nothing but arguments. I say we've had enough."

Or instead of admitting how they are contributing to the

mother's depression, family members might start making excuses for her: "She's just the melancholy type. There's nothing wrong with her or our family."

The best way to prevent the sabotaging of the counseling is to pace my probing. If I ask threatening questions too early or if I suggest changes too quickly, I'm likely to undermine my objectives.

● *Collusion*. Sometimes families can be gullible and believe anything a counselor says about the main counselee.

Consider this recent child-abuse case. A therapist saw a 4-year-old playing with anatomically correct dolls and doing so correctly; she obviously knew how people had intercourse. He assumed the child must have had intercourse with her father: how else could she have known?

When he explained this to the family, everyone thought it made sense and concluded the father was guilty.

Only after the court case was it learned that the father owned a porno shop on the side and would frequently bring home porno movies. Apparently the girl had surreptitiously seen a few of the movies. Exposure to porno movies may be a form of abuse, but it's significantly different than incest.

I mustn't assume that the family's diagnosis is correct just because they all happen to agree about the problem.

Stay Calm

Families are complex systems, and if I'm not careful, I can let the complexity get to me, making me anxious and tense. That not only harms me, it undercuts my counseling. So I have to remind myself to maintain a calm presence when I do family counseling.

It's especially easy to overreact when counseling with more than one member of the family at a time. Things can get out of hand too easily. Sometimes the family starts fighting; someone throws down a cup and says, "I'm getting out of here." Some couples who come for marital counseling seem to think that I am an audience they can fight in front of.

In such situations, I don't want to over-control things. If

you're just riding one horse and the horse pulls ahead, you don't have to do much to get it to slow down. But in driving six horses and one gets out of line, the temptation is to overcorrect. And that only causes more problems.

If an entire family starts blaming the father for his controlling behavior and the father starts to feel the weight of their criticism, I may be tempted to console the father, taking his side. If a rebellious teenager starts to attack his mom, I may want to come down on him for a bad attitude. If I were to counsel these people alone, I would have an easier time maintaining a empathetic but neutral stance.

I've found the best way to deal with the tendency to overreact and control is by working as much as possible with individuals one at a time. I break family problems into small components. I talk with each person individually.

Working with families, then, does not necessarily mean bringing the whole family together for counseling. That may be necessary, but I do that only after I've spent sufficient time with individual members to know what's going on in a family.

Getting the Family to Participate

All the above suggestions assume, of course, that one or more members of the family have agreed to become part of the counseling process. That, in many cases, is a big assumption. Still, a number of techniques can be employed to enlarge the scope of my counseling.

● *Prepare the counselee.* First I prepare the person I'm counseling. If I'm seeing a wife, and I conclude I need to see her husband, I might say, "I think I'm ready now to talk with your husband. But before I do, you should realize that the moment we involve another person's perspective, your problem may change a bit. Are you ready to discover that you may be contributing to the problem? Are you ready to find out a larger truth?"

Many counselees are not, in fact, ready to have others drawn in. One woman I counseled told me, "No. No. I don't want my husband involved. I don't want to hear how bad I am. I want you to work with me."

Some people are afraid of being discovered; that's especially true if the person coming is not the victim but the one coming to form an alliance with the therapist against the other party.

So first I've got to get the permission of the counselee before I involve others.

• *Create an alliance.* When I approach another family member, I try to create an alliance with the person I'm calling.

A distraught mother came in to see me about her 16-year-old daughter. The family was wealthy, and the girl had repeatedly crashed the car she was driving. The parents would give her a car, and she would have an accident in a couple of months. Then they would give her another car. The mother was getting more and more upset.

It was clear I had to talk with the daughter, so I called her and said, "Your mom has been seeing me for a couple of weeks now. But I need some other help to understand what's going on with her. Could you come in and give me your perspective?

"Okay," she replied. "I've noticed Mom has been upset lately. I probably should tell you what's been going on around here."

In this way, I formed a relationship with the daughter and together we had a common cause: to understand the mother.

Now the fact is, the daughter had to discover her role in the problems at home, but that was only possible after I had built a trusting relationship with her.

• *Use fear appropriately.* When the counselee's problem is serious and the family member resists coming in, I will build on any real fearfulness in the situation.

If I'm counseling a seriously depressed wife, I'll tell a husband reluctant to come in, "I am really concerned about your wife. She is quite depressed, and I need to give someone clear directions about what to do in case she decides to do the worst. I also need to know if she takes sleeping pills or if there's a gun around the house. I'd like you to come in and help me."

I would never exaggerate or lie. I don't want to manipulate people into my office. But if the situation has some danger — from a relationship being threatened to a possible suicide — I will mention it if I can't seem to convince another to come in.

No matter how I approach it, though, some people will simply not participate. In that case, I resign myself to working as best as I can with the counselee alone.

Long Expectations

Marjorie and her family, whom I discussed in the opening of the chapter, gradually pulled together again. They began to restructure the way they related to one another and now have found a new life. Her husband has a new job working for a Christian organization, and their granddaughter is the center of their lives.

To counsel such families is extremely gratifying. But sometimes I can't realistically expect that problems will be dealt with in a few months or even a few years.

Families resist change. They change very slowly. So in some cases, I look to the next generation as the place where family counseling will make its greatest impact.

I worked with one family where the husband, because of his upbringing, was often domineering toward his wife. The man's father never respected his own wife and treated her harshly. This man was repeating the pattern in his marriage.

I taught his wife how to better respond to him, and I suggested things the man might do differently. But I also saw that the man was never going to completely overcome this tendency.

So my next goal was to help the couple admit to their kids that this behavior was inappropriate and that the father was trying to change. I also encouraged them to teach their children how to live differently as they grew. In that way, they have a good chance of cutting the problem off at the father's generation.

In either case, no matter the stubbornness of family systems, determinism doesn't rule. Pastors can make a difference. With patience and reliance on the Holy Spirit, not only can individuals change but entire families as well, even to the next generation.

PART THREE

Problems Counseling Brings

I don't respond to every squeaky hinge as if it requires a major repair job. One drop of oil can do wonders.
— *Gary Gulbranson*

CHAPTER TEN

Fitting It In

The ring of the phone awoke me one Sunday morning at 5:30. A woman whom I had been counseling for some time tearfully asked me to drive to Billings Hospital in Chicago (some twenty-five miles away) and minister to her sister and brother-in-law. Their 2-year-old son had been in the bathtub the night before; while his mother was out of the room, his 8-year-old retarded sister had climbed into the tub and sat on him. When the mother returned, she found him in a coma.

When I received the call, it appeared the baby would die. With

Sunday's service before me I said, "I'll definitely go see them. But I have to see when I can work that into my schedule today. . . ."

"Pastor," she interrupted. "I think the little boy is going to die, and they need you right away."

"Okay. I'll be there shortly."

At six o'clock I phoned an elder and asked him to teach my 9:45 Bible class. I told him I expected to be back for the worship service at 11 A.M. Then I got into my car.

The woman was right: the boy did die, and the family desperately needed pastoral care. I spent several hours with them, drove back in time to preach the morning service, then returned to the hospital.

I could have handled this differently. When I received the phone call that morning, I could have told my counselee that I would contact a chaplain at the hospital. But from our sessions together, I knew she had been burned by authority figures in the past and thus distrusted them. I determined that her need to trust a pastor was higher than my responsibility to teach a class.

I regularly find myself in similar situations, weighing the cry for pastoral care against my other pastoral duties. Like a mother robin, standing worm in mouth before a nest full of gaping, chirping beaks, pastoral counselors often have a conflict of responsibilities. Who gets my limited supply of time and energy?

I have learned there are no neat solutions, but I can do several things to better balance the demands.

Manage Three Types of Care

When people and demands press me from every side, I sometimes feel as if I have little control over my schedule. But I do have control, and in varying degrees, depending on the type of care offered:

1. Scheduled care. I bunch my counseling toward the front of the week. After taking Monday off, I'm emotionally recharged, and with Sunday far enough away, I can devote my peak energies and concentration to the emotionally taxing work of counseling. I block off counseling hours on Tuesday and Wednesday in the morning and evening, with study sandwiched in the afternoon.

Over this type of care I can exert the most control. As long as the situation is not a crisis, I ask people to call my secretary, who schedules people into a fifty-minute session as soon as an opening is available.

At the back door after a church service, I said to one man who seemed upset, "Is there anything I can do for you?"

He answered, "I need to see you."

I said, "My secretary is the best one to schedule that. If you call tomorrow, she can find a spot for you on Tuesday or Wednesday."

He replied, "No, I need to see you now."

A few minutes later, after I had finished greeting the congregation, I went to the office with him. He was under heavy stress on the job, and it had come to a head for him that morning when he and his wife fought about his work.

We talked briefly, and then I said, "Bill, I'm glad I took the time today to understand what you're going through. I think I can be of real help to you. I am going to have a block of time available on Tuesday to deal with it. If you could call my secretary tomorrow, we'll work this thing out."

It turned out, he never made an appointment. Simply knowing that I was available to him and could give him focused attention if he needed it relieved some of his tension. He and his wife worked it out on their own.

2. *Schmooze care.* This is counseling by walking around, like the one-minute manager, and it obviates many scheduled appointments. I give schmooze care before and after church services, in the hallways during the week as activities are going on in the building, and over the phone.

Some of our older ladies meet several times monthly for a luncheon, and I sit in. This shows I consider them VIP's. Many problems of the elderly result from feeling nobody cares. We're a young congregation, and they know I wrestle with lots of family problems. If I didn't make myself available at a time like this luncheon, some would feel they were imposing to ask for my attention.

After a church service, schmooze care lets people know that I notice their presence. It means using or asking names, a handshake with eye-contact, and occasionally a discreet but pointed question.

If the person and I need to talk in private, I promise a phone call. Since people often want to schedule an entire counseling session to discuss what requires only five minutes, schmooze care can reduce appointments by trolling for problems that can be dealt with briefly.

Schmooze care works as effective follow-up. Without violating privacy I can say, "I haven't forgotten your situation. Is everything working out? I want you to know I'm still praying for you." I'm communicating that, in the midst of all these faces on Sunday morning, I remember their needs and that I still care.

3. Squeaky-hinge care. In the middle of one early morning elders meeting, the phone rang. A young woman whom I had been advising about buying a house had just learned her financing might fall through, and she was in a panic. I told her, "I can't discuss the situation right now, but I'll call you back later." That satisfied her.

This wasn't an emergency that merited calling me out of an elders' meeting, but it did merit some response. I have learned that all of us see our own needs as serious, never minor. We naturally want prompt attention.

So I have instructed my secretary to put callers through to me if they appear to be in a crisis, but I don't respond to every squeaky hinge as if it requires a major repair job. One drop of oil can do wonders.

Handling Trust Tests

Trust tests aggravate the problem of balancing counseling with my other responsibilities. In a society with few commitments, people establish trust slowly. Even in a church, people are not sure they can trust the pastor, and consciously or unconsciously, they sometimes test us.

The most common test happens in the counseling session.

Counselees generally don't reveal their deepest needs in initial sessions; instead they excavate less threatening sinkholes to see how I respond. If I pass those tests, they dig a little deeper.

Usually tests are stated obliquely. I was counseling one woman about various problems in her marriage. One day she said, "Someone needs to confront my husband about what he's doing."

I knew her well enough to know what she was really saying: "Pastor, I think you need to go and confront my husband. I want to know if you care enough about what's happening in my marriage and family to go and intervene yourself rather than sending elders or staff."

I've learned to be sensitive to subtle cues. Sometimes a trust test comes as a call to my home, ostensibly seeking information, actually checking if I'm available: *Can I reach him if I really need him?* People won't usually tell us if we fail a test. They just don't entrust themselves to us. They keep a safe distance, hide their problems, or go to another church.

To pass a trust test, I don't necessarily need to do the thing that's being requested of me. But in any event, I want to be aware when I'm being tested, so that even if I decide not to respond as requested, I'll be able to clearly communicate that I'm trustworthy: "I'm concerned about your husband's behavior too. But I've found that if I intervene in marriages as you're suggesting, I cause more harm than good. Is there another way we can deal with your husband?"

Some tests I don't want to pass. After a while, pastors can sense when someone is just trying to manipulate his or her attention. With such people, it is, in fact, better to fail the trust test — although with manipulators it's less a trust test than it is a test to see who's in charge. With such people, I do more harm than good by responding to their every plea.

Trust tests are so important that I've learned to deal with even perceived failures of trust. If someone is disappointed in my performance or out of line in their expectations, I address it as quickly as possible, preventing it from festering.

Three minutes before a Sunday morning worship service, a

church member approached me in the hall. She was broken up. "I just found out," she said, "that my oldest son has AIDS." He was in the hospital, and she assumed he was going to stay there. She didn't ask me to go see him, but she told me where the hospital was, tipping me off that she wanted me to do more than pray.

After the service I talked to her again and promised to visit him. On Monday I phoned him at the hospital, not wanting to trigger defensiveness with a surprise visit. I reached him, but he was just checking out.

On Tuesday night his mother, quite angry, went to a home Bible study and said to the group, "Pastor promised he would visit my son, but he didn't. This church hasn't helped me when I needed it."

When word reached me, I immediately called her at work. I told her that I understood she was disappointed in me, and I asked, "Has there ever been a time when I've told you I would do something that I didn't?"

"No," she replied.

"I may not have met your expectations, but I did call your son. And I arranged to meet him later in the week at his work."

She apologized. "I was upset and anxious over the whole situation. What I said wasn't fair, and I'm sorry."

After recognizing the issue of trust, there are several ways we can begin to balance our counseling load with our other responsibilities.

Get Counselees to Help

Counseling can feel like a lonely job, especially if I'm the one who alone has to rein in my schedule. However, over the years I've found some help: I've learned that the majority of callers will help me manage my schedule if I recruit them as allies.

With people unfamiliar with counseling, I offer a little orientation. After their problems are on the table, I say, for example, "We meet for fifty minutes each week. We will need four sessions to get a handle on this issue. If we haven't begun to resolve things by then, we'll decide together whether we should refer you to someone else who can help you."

Then they understand that such boundaries are not arbitrary rules but boundaries within which we can work effectively. Once they understand that, they get down to business more quickly.

I often ask people to plan ahead for our session. They write an agenda and keep a record of areas in which they've been seeking improvement. Thus they arrive focused, mentally prepared, able to address problems more thoroughly. This increases the comfort quotient on both sides, since I know they won't waste time, and they know what to expect.

When another responsibility intrudes, I sometimes enlist the help of counselees by telling them what's happened. Sometimes this changes the whole dynamic of the relationship.

I had been counseling one young woman for several weeks. Just before she came in for her appointment, I received a call from a family who had just had a death. While I didn't have to rush off at that moment, it was heavy on my mind. When the young woman walked in, she said, "You look troubled today, pastor."

"I have to say that I am," I replied. "I just heard from a family who lost a loved one. I'm going to spend time with them this afternoon. I'm concerned about them."

She replied immediately, "My situation can wait. Why don't you go see that family. Is there anything I can do to help?" Before leaving, she prayed for the family and for my ministry to them.

Teach the Church How to Counsel

A bracing fact of counseling life: the better we are at it, the more that needy people will crowd our small doorstep. The more people sense we are trustworthy and caring, the more clanking skeletons they will pull out of the closet.

I regard hurting people who call on me as my responsibility. But as Moses learned from Jethro, my responsibility isn't to counsel everyone but to ensure that counseling gets done. Since my church understands this principle, we seek ways to spread the load.

For instance, we offer a Tuesday night Circle of Concern, in which people gather each week for a month to learn about a particular problem (child abuse, eating disorders, alcoholism, and the like). We also teach systematic helping skills at these meetings.

We have developed a list of proven helping agencies and counselors in the community to which we regularly refer people.

In addition, we train lay counselors and invest in staff members with counseling gifts. Recently we paid for our youth pastor and his wife to receive some formal training to augment their ministry with high school age, college age, and many single members.

Preaching is a key time to equip people for counseling ministry. I prepare my sermons to be useful not only to people in trouble but also to those who will be helping such people. My sermons often include point-by-point application: "Here are five things to do when you are depressed." "Here are six steps for getting out of financial troubles." I encourage listeners to take notes and to share the sermon ideas with others.

At holidays, for example, I will say from the pulpit, "During special holidays, people expect more than ever that they will find some happiness. Instead of taking away some of their depression, though, holidays often make matters worse. During holidays, in fact, I often have an increased counseling load. But there are some things that you can do to encourage others at this time of year." Then I list some ways to help.

Maintain Healthy Attitudes

Planning and scheduling and delegating will not help me handle the pressure if I'm harboring bad attitudes about my hectic ministry. To counter that regular temptation, I've learned to nurture three traits.

• *Forgiveness.* A young man whom I had helped recover from a divorce was grateful. Unfortunately he was so grateful that he wanted to deepen our friendship socially beyond what was possible for me. Without my knowledge, he even made me a beneficiary of his life insurance policy. When he finally realized such a friendship wasn't possible, he was deeply disappointed and stopped attending the church. All this I found out from a mutual friend.

The news triggered some anger in me; I don't like to let people down. I was angry at myself for not picking up the signals and heading off this problem, angry at my overloaded schedule, and angry at him for his expectations.

Even though people's expectations are sometimes unreasonable, I'm still troubled when I can't meet them. I've had to learn to forgive myself for not being superhuman. Even then, sometimes I still end up carrying some resentment against the people who've expected the unreasonable, and I've had to learn to forgive them.

One couple whom I counseled gave me a marble stone etched with the words "A happy marriage is the union of two good forgivers." Forgiveness is equally important for happily balanced pastors.

● *Flexibility*. A pastor is a general practitioner. I move from sermon preparation, to premarriage counseling, to board meetings, to the funeral home. If I cannot shift gears easily, I'll have trouble.

Sometimes, in order to do counseling at night, I leave the office early, pick up my daughter at school, and spend time with her and the rest of my family. I schedule most of our elder meetings for early mornings so that evenings are available for family or other work.

● *Creativity*. Rather than counseling engaged couples two by two, I organize them into a premarriage counseling group that meets on Saturday morning. That's what I mean by creativity — trying to approach an old problem in a new way.

Another example: I wanted to give singles a model of family life to consider, and I wanted to meet some of their many counseling needs. So my wife and I sponsored a weekly evening Bible study in our home for nearly a year. Twenty single-parents, some with children, met in our house over that period, enabling me to minister while being with my family.

When it comes to balance, counseling pastors resemble a halfback in football. Sometimes as the back runs up the sideline, a tackler shoves him hard enough to force him out of bounds, but the leaning halfback is able to tightrope a few more steps inside the field of play before his imbalance causes him to step over the line.

Likewise, I may be able to dash for a while with my ministry out of balance, but eventually I'll hit the turf unless I can regain my center of gravity.

My goal is to remain balanced so I can maintain my ministry of counseling to those in need. I don't want so to overextend myself that I fall out of bounds. A balanced ministry will be an ongoing ministry.

Sexual responsiveness is fundamentally instinctual. The basic attraction to others should not concern us. What we do with the attraction is what is important.

— *Archibald Hart*

CHAPTER ELEVEN

Transference: Loosening the Tie That Blinds

If you were hungry for love, wouldn't it be nice to find someone who was educated, mannerly, articulate but also a good listener, respected in the community, occupationally powerful, yet unselfish and willing to spend time alone with you for free?

Numbers of counselees think so. They come to a church office and find themselves in the presence of the kindest, most receptive, admirable, gentle, wise person they've met in a long time. The solution to their turmoil, they gradually realize, is not so much what the pastor says as the pastor himself.

In the doctor of ministry classes I teach, I talk about this hazard, technically known as "transference" (the client projecting unmet feelings and desires into the counseling relationship, feelings and desires that belong somewhere else). The students each term write a response paper on how the course has related to their situations. Every time, 20 to 25 percent of them report transference as a problem they have faced in their ministries.

Countertransference, the even more distressing corollary, is when the *counselor* projects unmet feelings and desires into the mix that belong elsewhere.

The Problem

At the outset, let me stress that an intimate but inappropriate relationship between a pastor and a church member does not always involve physical sex. Although such relationships have the potential to become sexual, they may remain as emotional attachments for a long time. (This is especially true of female pastors.)

"I've been lonely," wrote one male pastor, "and I cannot communicate with my wife. She doesn't understand how I feel. All she wants to talk about are the kids and her mother. I want to explore ideas, thoughts, and feelings. So I began spending time with this other woman after we finished our counseling sessions. She understands me. I can share myself with her. I hope this doesn't go further — I'd hate to have to decide whether to leave my wife."

The relationship was only emotional at that point. But such a relationship *will* go further if the counselor does nothing to stop it. All sexual affairs begin in this benign way.

Although most liaisons emerge out of counseling relationships, some start when a minister has to work closely with someone on a committee or project. Since more and more younger women have assumed church responsibilities in recent years, male ministers are now in closer working relationships with women, where feelings of warmth and affection can easily arise. Sometimes the relationship develops with a secretary or other colleague.

Male pastors are typically attracted to younger women, although it is not unusual for ministers to be attracted to older ones as well. And attraction does not require extensive contact. Glances from the pulpit or a chance encounter in a corridor or on a hospital visit can trigger a strong attraction to another.

Transference for female pastors can have other dimensions as well. Female pastors can be the target of seductive ploys by certain types of males. These men are usually out to prove their masculinity; they see the "pure" female pastor as a challenge to conquer, especially if she is attractive. Whether she is married doesn't seem to matter.

Female pastors also attract very strong emotional transferences from other females. These women want to be "special" friends, and some of these transferences can be obsessional, demanding a lot of attention from the pastor.

Basic attraction to others should not concern us. It is a normal part of human life. Sexual responsiveness is fundamentally instinctual, though it is heavily influenced by learning. It is based in biology, in hormones that can powerfully control behavior and emotions.

What we do with the attraction is what's important. Whether we succumb to it, deny or repress it (which is often the gateway to increased vulnerability later on), or honestly and courageously deal with the attraction will be determined not only by our spiritual maturity but also by our level of self-understanding and professional competence.

The apostle Paul says, "It is God's will that you should be holy; that you should avoid sexual immorality; that each of you should learn to control his own body in a way that is holy and honorable, not in passionate lust like the heathen, who do not know God" (1 Thess. 4:3–5).

In essence, Paul tells us to understand our bodies and know how to control our urges and drives. Since much attraction gets out of hand in avoidable situations, and often arising out of needs the average pastor does not understand, better training about the counseling process can prevent the catastrophe of ministerial affairs.

Where Transference Happens

I believe one main source of church-related sexual affairs starts in the counseling relationship. The transference and countertrans-ference that emerge in counseling get out of control.

Over the past two decades, the topic of sexual intimacies with clients has received considerable attention in the helping profes-sions. In California it is illegal (not just unethical) for a psychothera-pist to have sex with a client, even if evidence shows the client was the primary seducer and a willing participant. Psychotherapists are required to report all cases of clients who report sexual encounters with previous psychotherapists.

These professions readily acknowledge that in the close, per-sonal relationship of psychotherapy, warm, friendly, intimate feel-ings are bound to develop. Just as surgery produces blood, therapy produces a closeness that can easily be mislabeled "love." The competent therapist recognizes these feelings as a by-product of therapy and is trained to deal with them. His or her own hangups and unmet needs are not allowed to enter the picture.

True, not all psychotherapists are adequately trained or fol-low their training. But some ministers are not even aware of these issues, let alone have training in dealing with them. Both need help.

Although a minister's married life is a basic deterrent to seeking an illicit affair, it does not guarantee safety in the counsel-ing room or the more subtle encounters of committee or project work.

I have always believed, despite protests from unsuspecting pastors, that a minister's vulnerability has nothing to do with his marital happiness. (My experience in this area is mainly with mar-ried, male pastors; thus the masculine pronouns throughout this article.) For many centuries Scripture has warned us to be on guard when we feel most safe! Sexual attraction can occur as easily when one is happily married as when one is not. You may more deliber-ately *seek out* an affair when you are not happy, but you are not necessarily safe when all is bliss at home.

Contributing Factors

All ministers are vulnerable to affairs for the following reasons:

- *The counseling relationship.* Counseling provides an opportunity to explore the feelings of another person. People not involved in counseling don't get the same opportunity and probably can't grasp how deeply satisfying a truly empathic understanding can be.

I know some ministers who deliberately refuse all one-to-one counseling with the opposite sex; they avoid the intimacy of counseling because they know they are too needful of intimacy themselves and thus subject to temptation. In such cases, avoiding counseling is a sensible decision.

● *The pastoral image.* Ministers, because of their role, can be especially attractive to members of the opposite sex. They are perceived as caring, concerned, and helpful, yet with a power that is exciting. They can attract pretty women who in other settings would not give them a second look. Many ministers confuse this attraction to their role with attraction to their person.

They are also perceived as safe. Intimate conversations with ministers do not typically create as much guilt as do such conversations with others: "After all, if the pastor is willing, it can't be that bad," they rationalize. Many are misled into believing they can allow their warm, loving feelings to develop with a minister because the pastor will know where and when to set limits.

When they find no such limits set, they often panic. In other words, the minister, having stepped out of the pastoral role, no longer seems attractive; that pastor has destroyed the very reason for the attraction and suddenly faces an accuser.

● *The denial of sexual urges.* It is an unfortunate consequence of our Christian aspirations to holiness that we create a sexually repressive subculture. Many ministers (and Christians in general) fear their sexuality and see in it a tremendous potential for sin. Although they are fundamentally right, the healthier way to deal with the sex drive is to bring it into the open and courageously confront and master it.

The majority of ministers enter their profession with the highest ethical intentions. They deeply desire to be genuine and spiritual. And many are also confused and troubled about their sexuality, especially when their sexual feelings seem contrary to their high calling. Rather than confronting their feelings by admitting to another the power and pervasiveness of sexual urges, some pastors repress them, diverting their sexual energies into work or a hobby. Others simply deny they even have sexual urges toward other women.

Repression and denial, particularly in male pastors, can lead them to believe that they are immune to sexual temptations, and so they increase their vulnerability. They end up counseling women alone in their homes or working closely with women late into the night, believing they have things under control. When the inevitable finally happens, everyone is shocked. But due to their lack of openness in this area, their traditional role and high moral standards have ended up fortifying their march into sin.

● *The home situation.* Although a happy marriage does not guarantee safety, an unhappy one certainly doesn't help. "The pain of having a lack of intimacy and free flow of conversation in my marriage was too much to bear," one pastor wrote me. "I longed to love with abandon, to feel feelings and share intimacies with someone else." He went on to describe a series of seven affairs over ten years.

Although such excessive needs for affection can be neurotic, if a marriage is satisfying, a minister should be able to focus even his neurotic needs on his spouse. An affair can easily be encouraged when the need for intimacy is great and the marriage does not provide an opportunity for close sharing.

● *Life stages.* It is quite clear that men, in particular, are more vulnerable to affairs when they pass through critical stages of life. One of these is commonly called the midlife crisis, but there are other critical stages as well. Almost every decade brings its own period of crisis, demanding a major adjustment of values and behavior.

Ministers do not escape these. If their work is not satisfying, or if they are having problems in the church, they are more prone to temptation in a crisis period. In times of burnout or interpersonal conflict, or when major life decisions must be made, the desire for comfort and emotional closeness increases dramatically.

Recognizing the Danger Signals

Since an intimate affair can develop during counseling almost unnoticed, a discussion of the danger signals of countertransference is crucial.

1. The pastor begins to look forward to the counseling sessions with a particular parishioner. He or she ruminates about the appointment and cannot wait for the time to arrive. Pulse rate increases, palms become sweaty, and the voice develops a slight tremor when the parishioner arrives.

2. Very soon the pastor begins to extend the session time and may even grant extra counseling sessions. The minister cancels other appointments to please the parishioner (often without even realizing what's happening).

3. Hidden or oblique messages are sent both ways. The message, which on the surface is innocuous, means something more personal at a deeper level: "I really enjoy my time with you, Pastor" or "Your wife (husband) is sure lucky to have you as a husband (wife)."

4. Counseling sessions may spend an inordinate amount of time on sexual matters. The client may begin to share sexual history or previous affairs that are unrelated to the problem for which counseling has been sought.

5. The pastor may begin to notice more his or her own marital frustrations. Such pastors begin to complain about petty things, often because they feel guilty and can alleviate their guilt by transforming it into anger.

6. The pastor begins to fantasize excessively and then exclusively about the client.

7. He makes excuses to call her and have extra conversations with her. Luncheon appointments in a remote setting may then follow. These are rationalized as "additional counseling sessions."

8. Casual touching becomes more frequent, and the sessions end with embraces that become more prolonged or intense.

One particular personality type is particularly risky for the male minister: the female hysterical personality. This person is typically shallow, overly reactive, even vivacious, uninhibited in displaying sexuality, given to flirtations, coquetry, and romantic fantasy. Such a person is also impressionable and craves excitement but is naive and frigid. She is, in essence, a caricature of femininity, drawing attention to herself to obtain admiration.

Because this personality is extremely prone to transference, the pastor who falls prey to her seductions is bound to be destroyed. He may be embarrassed by public displays of affection and the discovery that her initial attractiveness was only superficial.

It has long been recognized in psychiatry and psychology that the difference between a brilliant and an average therapist is that the former recognizes the hysterical personality and runs away faster. This should also be true for brilliant ministers!

Dealing with Transference

The average pastor cannot afford the time and energy demanded by a counselee with a high propensity for transference. Training in dealing with transference requires extensive supervision, far more than is typically provided in a course on counseling. If this training is available, you should take advantage of it.

In the meantime:

● *Treat it like other feelings.* The safest way to deal with transference is simply to receive it as one would receive any feeling of a client. This is done without encouraging the transference any further. The counselor helps the client see that the feelings reside in the counselee, not in the counselor.

The counselor may ask clarifying questions to increase the client's understanding of his or her feelings. "You feel you're in love with me. Why do you suppose this is so?" In other words, the full expression of feelings is allowed without either condoning or rejecting them.

● *Be direct about it,* although this should be done only at a later stage, and only when it can be done without offending the client. For example, "Sometimes when people share their innermost secrets with someone else, they feel drawn and very close to that person. Do you think this is what is happening here?"

● *Always stay professional.* I don't mean you cannot be friendly and personable. I do mean that you keep to your appointment schedule and avoid stepping out of your professional role.

● *Refer hard cases.* Don't hesitate to make a referral to a trusted Christian psychotherapist if the transference gets out of hand. A mark of professional competence is knowing your limits.

The Pastor's Protection

But what about countertransference? What does a pastor do with those warm, loving feelings toward a client?

● *Never share these feelings with your counselee.* Never talk of them or even hint they are present. They are your problem, not your client's. If you do, you will either encourage an intimate relationship, or you will be rejected. You lose both ways.

● *Understand the difference between countertransference and simple attraction.* In simple attraction, which is normal, you can walk away from the person to whom you feel some attraction. You are free to leave. You can choose to leave physically and mentally. But when you are obsessed with someone, when you allow yourself to think about the client constantly, you have problems. You must learn to redirect your thoughts and avoid fantasizing over the person.

● *Be aware of your needs for intimacy.* Maintain an intimate relationship with your spouse and another close friend or two. Ministers are often lonely people, and they sometimes shut themselves off from others. By so doing they will likely at some point find themselves craving intimacy, praise, or admiration. When this happens, get help.

● *Develop a system of accountability.* Not only are you accountable to God, but you need someone to whom you can be accountable and talk frankly about your feelings. Such a person could be a work colleague, a pastor from another church (to whom the accountability can be reciprocated), or even your spouse.

The Marital Relationship

In fact, the spouse's role is crucial in helping a pastor develop a safe position from which to counsel.

For instance, in terms of male pastors, many wives find it difficult to understand how their husbands, as pastors, can be attracted to other women. How can a man so prominent, so respected, so intelligent, be subject to vulgar temptation?

As Paul Tournier points out in his book *To Understand Each Other*, this attitude only increases a pastor's guilt feelings and prevents him from sharing his innermost struggles over sex with her. To him, she becomes the incarnation of moral law.

Tournier says, "This is the driving force of much adultery, so severely denounced by the virtuous . . . wife once she discovers it." She thinks that if he really loved her, he would not think of other women.

What she doesn't know is that her pastor/husband desperately wants to confide this struggle to her. He wants to channel his arousal back to her, where it belongs. But sometimes her veil of silence, resistance, and condemnation only increases the emotional distance.

In other cases, it's ministers who build walls around themselves, refusing to let their spouses see their intimate thoughts and feelings. Many pastors are introverts who only with difficulty can talk about their feelings. Or ministers may be plagued by guilt, because a good minister, they think, should be able to conquer such temptations.

Then again, some pastors don't want to burden their spouses with their own struggles. Or others, so tired from listening to other people's troubles day after day, have for some time abandoned the idea of intently engaging their spouse in conversation.

Whether the lack of intimacy is created by one or both partners, however, the solution is the same: the couple needs to build a safer, more secure marriage in which they both — particularly in this case, the minister — can talk openly about their fears, sufferings, sorrows, guilt, and misery.

Although he writes to male ministers, Tournier's advice on this matter works both ways: "The best protection against sexual temptations is to be able to speak honestly of them and to find, in the wife's understanding, without any trace of complicity whatsoever, effective and affective help needed to overcome them.''

Coupled with a dependence upon God's Holy Spirit to provide help in time of trouble, this sort of transparency can prevent affairs. It can also build a depth of love, understanding, and oneness that I doubt can be experienced any other way this side of heaven.

Pastors are caretakers, a characteristic of those who answer the call to ministry. We need to be needed. In that sense, perhaps we're all a little codependent, making caregiving an emotional hazard of our profession.

— Jim Smith

CHAPTER TWELVE
Maintaining Your Psychological Balance

My prayer was neither theologically nor politically correct. With my green Chevy Vega idling at the corner of Mockingbird and Greenville in Dallas, Texas, I broke down. "Lord, I'm the only thing that stands between these people and hell," I prayed shamelessly. "They'll have to go to hell 'cause I'm going home. I quit."

When I had left the office that evening, my secretary had apprised me of my eight-month waiting list and the forty or so phone calls screaming for my attention. I was overwhelmed by it all, tyrannized and oppressed by the guilt. Playing the role of messiah had taken its toll. Like the lifeguard who gets pulled under while rescuing a drowning victim, my workaholism was dragging my own emotional health under water.

Pastors are susceptible to emotional fatigue. Yet the minister's emotional health is indispensable for effective counseling and longevity in the profession. Historically, pastors are caretakers. We need to be needed. And in that sense, perhaps we're all a little codependent, making caregiving an emotional hazard of our profession.

I've discovered since this crisis that the psychological hazards of counseling can be avoided. A meaningful and ongoing prayer life, of course, is the central element to a pastor's psychological health. Prayer not only puts our ministries into perspective, it is the means by which we are given divine strength and wisdom to do the work God has called us to.

In addition to prayer, I've found a few other practices also help.

Monitor Your Pulse

Just like the pulse needs to be checked at the beginning of a physical, so does the pastor's psychological pulse. I monitor my psychological pulse by asking myself a series of questions.

• *Am I emotionally available at home?* The inability to be emotionally present with my wife, Jan, or my daughters is a good indicator I'm on relational overload. If on the drive home from work, I find myself hoping and praying they've had a good day so I don't have to hold the bucket for their tears, my emotional tank is on empty.

And if I'm watching TV, tearing up over a plot not warranting my weeping and sobbing, I'm emotionally needy. I don't have enough emotional reserve to take it in stride. It may be a tragic plot, for example, where a parent is abusive to a child. Under healthy conditions, though, I'd be angry at the parent: "What a rat! You fink!" But if I'm emotionally breaking up over it, that's a reliable barometer about the plight of my soul.

• *Am I snookered?* Getting "snookered," or hooked, is counseling jargon, at least at our church, for letting your own concerns cloud and distort the counseling process.

Growing up in an alcoholic family, I played the role of protecting my mother. As an alcoholic, my father was verbally and emotionally abusive to my mother. So my tendency in marital counseling, if I'm out of balance, is to unconsciously side with the woman against the man. I feel more empathy for the woman; I lose objectivity. Getting snookered may indicate my own emotional needs are on the skids.

• *Am I abusing power?* Power is endemic to pastoral counseling. But the misuse of power, like leveraging clients for your own needs, is evidence of psychological sickness.

Not long ago, I could have quadrupled my money overnight in the stock market simply because I heard some inside information from one of my clients. That's never been a serious temptation to me. But information about businesses and families is privy to pastors, and we need to beware of the temptation to cozy up to people for financial rewards or perks.

Counseling pastors are entrusted with a wealth of information about their clients. Manipulating them with potentially damaging information is unethical and unprofessional.

• *Am I voyeuristic?* Voyeurism means gaining sexual gratification from a safe distance. By asking questions irrelevant to the counseling process, pastors can become voyeurs, using the guise of counseling to gratify their unmet needs.

If I'm counseling a couple, for example, and the husband complains the wife is not freed up sexually, I need more information to understand what he means by that. Does it mean she dresses in the closet? Or does it mean she won't use whipping cream and swing from the chandelier? I need to ask appropriate questions to help them work through their issues, but not the sort of questions that titillate my own sexual curiosity.

If I start asking questions for my arousal, I've become voyeuristic, which removes me from a position of healing.

• *Am I believing my own press releases?* There are people who demand to see only me. They believe I'm the only person in the world who can help them. At our church, we call it the Hem-of-the-

Garment Syndrome: "If I could just touch the hem of Jim's garment . . . " The humor helps us keep perspective. But it's serious business. If you start believing you alone have the answers for all the world's problems, you've crossed over the line of what makes for psychological balance.

● *Is my level of what's acceptable diminishing?* After constantly counseling D-minus marriages, it's easy for me to start believing that a C-plus relationship is not that bad. If I'm emotionally spent and listening to a couple drone on about their marriage, unconsciously I could begin to muse, *Why are you so uptight? Your C-plus marriage is better than most!* I lose hope for the A-plus marriage that God offers them. God's ideals, then, become a casualty of my emotional overload.

Setting Limits

Maintaining emotional equilibrium also requires that I set personal limits in five areas.

1. I have to recognize the number of clients I can emotionally handle each week. For myself, I've noticed that if I counsel six clients per day, I'm fine. If I do seven, I'm marginal. But if I see eight, I'm dead — I've hit emotional overload, and then my soul takes a nose dive. Time for legitimate emergencies and crises also need to be figured into my weekly schedule.

2. I put a ceiling on the number of draining cases in my counseling load. Many psychologists will not work with more than two borderline personality disorders at one time. That's wise advice for the counseling pastor. Their constant depression can easily sabotage the emotional condition of the pastor.

3. I balance my counseling load with clients I truly enjoy working with. I couldn't do just crisis intervention and survive. My first love is teaching, and so I would rather school clients on how to have marital intimacy than to constantly mop up the aftermath. I'm not much of a sewer cleaner. And so I keep a lid on the cases that drain me emotionally and balance the rest of my load, as much as possible, with what I love to do the most.

4. I create artificial barriers between me and my ministry. My

secretary is an artificial barrier, my insulation from the instant demands of hurting people. She's like the wicked witch of Endor: no one sees me until they sneak past her! I'm too nice to people. She, on the other hand, is direct with those who would encroach upon my schedule.

Another barrier may be screening the phone calls at home with an answering machine, or simply taking the phone off the hook. Ready statements like "Why don't you call the office tomorrow" or "I need to check my calendar" also serve to buffer the pastor against the barrage of needy people.

5. I refuse to accept my client's problems as my own. I always delineate whose problem is whose.

Recently, a teenage boy kicked out of the house by his parents and with no place to go camped out in my office. I felt as if he was waiting for me to locate a place for him to stay. If I had gotten on the phone and tried to find him a place to stay, I would have rescued him.

And though I hurt for him — the poor guy was obviously scared — I consciously refused. We finally decided he should check into a motel at his expense.

"Well, there's the phone," I announced. So he called the motel and reserved a room until things cooled down at home.

When a person comes and complains about not having a job, my temptation is to call someone I know and try to help the person find work. I musn't do that, because then it becomes my problem.

Instead, I'll say, "Let's talk about some options. But it's your job to go and find a job. I can't do that for you."

Occasionally that's a tough line to define. Sometimes people really do need financial help. Sometimes there's a legitimate need — for example, a husband has just walked off and left a wife and children without any resources. Those people we do help.

But a lot of people just want to come in and feel better. And there's a tremendous temptation to free people from their pain. But there's efficacy in pain; pain is a great teacher. By refusing to alleviate their pain, we strengthen them in the healing process and safeguard the emotional well-being of our soul as well. If I get sucked into their problems, I can't be a counselor.

Finding a Soul to Lean On

Ongoing supervision for the counselor is another fundamental to long-term emotional health.

At our counseling center, we supervise each other. In addition, I meet monthly with three different friends in psychology to discuss my cases. We never name names, of course; that would violate confidentiality. But we are specific about details. (In the counselee's intake sheet, we clearly spell out to them that outside consultation may be necessary.)

Often I've encouraged pastors to find a mental health professional, so that every couple of weeks or once a month, they can get the perspective of a veteran psychologist on their cases.

For the rural pastor, that's impossible. Other local ministers, however, make competent supervisors, even if they are from a theologically "foreign" denomination. And even a mature friend, with little or no psychology background, can offer acumen and perspective on counseling cases.

Accountability, as much as supervision, is another reason why ministers need a soul mate, whether close friend or spouse. Especially with a spouse, though, the pastor must be careful not to poison the spouse's attitude toward individuals in the congregation. Confidentiality still demands the anonymity of the client, even from a spouse.

How much you do share with your spouse, however, depends on the size of your congregation. Since our church is quite large and my wife, Jan, is mostly uninvolved in the ministry, I feel comfortable in sharing some of my counseling situations with her, especially the humorous ones. It draws her into my world, giving her a sense of what I have to contend with on a regular basis.

Sexual accountability, however, is a different ball game. Divulging an attraction for a client may be too threatening for some spouses. "I've got a parishioner who creates fantasy problems for me; she and I need to be held accountable" is a confession for the ears of a colleague, not a marriage partner.

Relational overload and fatigue can make the counseling pastor especially vulnerable to sexual temptations, especially when his or her own emotional needs are unmet. In such situations, counseling relationships can drift unsuspectingly towards a sexual ambush. Admitting sexual temptations to a trustworthy friend, though, takes the sting and the mystery out of the attraction.

Accountability bolsters the resolve of pastors, keeping them apprised of their own needs and alert for psychological duplicity.

A Constant Sense of Growing

In the ministry, our walk with the Lord can be easily sacrificed to the urgent; this is especially true in pastoral counseling. Often we become so busy that we forget to nurture our own spiritual needs. A constant sense of spiritual growth, though, forces us to confront our own issues. We don't have to be perfectly whole before the Lord will use us. We do, however, need to be experiencing the presence of Christ in the hidden parts of our psyche.

Some ministers, believing themselves called by God, have ended up in the ministry for all the wrong reasons. In reality, the call of God may have been distorted by errant motives and childhood pain. But whatever the issues — sexual addictions, marital difficulties, or narcissistic personality tendencies — pastors, to be healthy, must be working through their own issues, experiencing firsthand God's healing in their own lives.

And it's this healthiness that makes for effective counseling in the long run. I know one former pastor, for instance, who during his pastoral ministry was distressed that not many came to see him for counseling. And when people did come, he was rarely successful at helping them work through their struggles.

Years later, he recognized that he had been hindered in counseling others because he himself had yet to work through the struggles he was having with intimacy. For some time he had been closing himself off from his wife, his church, and his friends, sharing less and less of himself with them. His people sensed his reserve and found it difficult to entrust themselves to him.

"If I had had a periodic checkup with another counselor myself, I think I would have seen this pattern earlier and dealt with it. As it was, my counseling ministry was handicapped. I missed an opportunity to help a lot more people."

Psychological health, to a large extent, is a matter of degrees. Emotional balance for the pastor, then, is not about personal perfection but a growing self-awareness.

Professional growth also contributes to my emotional condition. The field of human dysfunction is broad, and counseling pastors, to stay relevant, need continual professional development. The constant process of integrating psychology with what I understand biblically and theologically is food for my own psyche. That's why my monthly rendezvous with friends in psychology is so vital. A constant sense of professional maturation serves to maintain my sense of psychological health.

Redeeming Humor

Over the last twenty-five years of ministry, the prolonged exposure to the human predicament has sobered me. In a way, I suppose, pastoral counseling has scarred me. Seeing so much sadness and inhumanity has rubbed some of the shine off my disposition.

That's why humor is more important to me than ever. I'm convinced that a sense of humor can put some shine back in my disposition. It's another component critical to emotional equilibrium in the ministry.

Humor also cuts through the grimness and heaviness that envelopes the pastor when he's up to his eyeballs in needy parishioners. Part of a balanced approach to counseling, then, is looking for the folly in their pain — not in an insensitive way, of course.

One cartoon by Doug Hall shows a woman standing during a prayer meeting, praying, "Lord, I lay before you the prayer concerns voiced this morning . . . even though most of 'em sound like whining to me." That's how I feel about counselee's problems sometimes, and to see it put humorously defuses my frustration.

Humor also is a key not to taking myself too seriously. There's only one Messiah, and that position's already taken. Leith Anderson, pastor of Wooddale Church in Minneapolis, aptly puts the pastor's role into relief: "If somebody has a situation that absolutely demands that you attend to it in the next twenty-four hours, you're not capable of dealing with it anyway."

So I allow humor to become a regular part of my life. You can't force humor into your relationships and your way of thinking, but you can be open and receptive when it comes. When I'm with colleagues and we're discussing our cases, not everything has to be serious. We sometimes poke fun at each other and our clients and ourselves, and as long as we don't become flippant and sarcastic, the laughter that results is a healing balm.

I also try to set an atmosphere where humor is encouraged. In the reception area of my counseling office, I often place a book of cartoons for people to thumb through, offering them a humorous glimpse on our plight as humans. When people get to know me, they often send me cartoons and humorous ditties, and I encourage that.

We all have little quirks that besmirch our personalities and frustrations that get in the way of ministry. Chuckling at our human entanglements liberates us from taking ourselves too seriously. A healthy dose of humor allows the pastor not to lose sight of the forest while counseling in the trees.

Getting Away

Whether it's biking, golfing, or gardening, pastors should cultivate activities that divert their energies from ministry. That's even more true of those who do a lot of counseling.

My wife owns her own company and is not available on my regular day off. So on Thursdays, my day away from the grind, I hit the road with a fishing pole or if it's hunting season, a shotgun in my hand. So I'm either casting a line or in the field dressing a quail on my day of rest.

The great outdoors are a diversion for me. I find that my own emotional health requires activities that refresh and distract me from the constant drain of my clients. Sitting in a boat, wetting a worm and "yukking it up" with my friends, takes care of my needs.

When my friend Robbie comes to visit, we immediately head for the lake. It's our time to "laugh and scratch" and do all those male bonding things that fishermen do. Fishing and hunting are two pills that keep me in counseling ministry for the long haul.

My frightful prayer at that memorable corner in Dallas broke my workaholism and my fixation to be the messiah for everyone that came down the pike. It wasn't a dramatic turn — I didn't take a sabbatical or completely restructure my life and ministry. I just started to take one day at a time, one client at a time. I still struggle at times with the yearning to fix everybody's problems. But I've started paying more attention to my psychological health. And that, ironically, has helped me attend more effectively to the psychological health of others.

With the strong resemblance to family and home, it's not surprising that profound things happen in pastoral counseling.

— *Craig Brian Larson*

Epilogue

D oes any dimension of pastoral ministry so encompass the two hemispheres of soaring ideals and earthy reality as counseling? The hearts of pastoral counselors pound with compassion, healing, love, discipleship, wisdom, and comfort.

At the same time, they ache from exposure to bitterness, divorce, profanity, incest, hatred, adultery, death, cancer, and doubt. Like the mother of an infant, pastors spend their days singing the heartwarming songs of cradle and nursery while handling dirty diapers and messy bibs.

To put it another way: pastoral counselors know the church as a Christian *family*, in its holiness as well as its humanity.

That's been true of pastors since the beginning. Paul, for instance, likened himself to both a mother and a father to the Thessalonians.

He ascribed to himself the motherly (and godly) trait of loving-kindness, and in these pages we have read much of the pastoral counselor's need for patience, listening, empathy, mercy. In the pastor's office the sick are nursed, the hungry fed, the tearful soothed, the simple taught.

Like a father, Paul characterized his ministry as encouraging the downhearted, comforting the afflicted, and urging the straying child to walk worthy of God — another realistic portrait of a counselor's task. In their pastor, counselees find strength, challenge, wisdom, discipline, maturity.

With the strong resemblance to family and home, it is not surprising that profound things happen in pastoral counseling. Deep emotions. Tears. Healing. Growth. There people see a feeble, nonetheless real, reflection of the Wonderful Counselor: "Come to me all you who are weary and burdened, and I will give you rest. Take my yoke upon you and learn from me, for I am gentle and humble in heart, and you will find rest for your souls."